Live a Better Life
Your Best Life

And Make the World a Better Place

DAVID M MASTERS

For more information contact:

David M Masters

% Assembly of CEH

1673 S. Market Blvd, #143

Chehalis, WA 98532

Tel. 360-538-5809

www.davidmmasters.com

Cover Photo by Volodymyr Goinyk

ISBN: 1537626582
ISBN-13: 978-1537626581

DEDICATION

This book is dedicated to my children and grandchildren, whom without their love and support, I might not have another reason to live besides my love of helping others achieve their highest and best.

I honor PFC Aaron Fairbairn for his sacrifice in Afghanistan for his country and every other man and woman in service who face the potential of paying the ultimate price on behalf of the rest of us. Thank you for your service.

So, I also dedicate this volume to those who are taking the steps to take their own individual high road of love to a better life and are ready to make the world a better place.

This book is for you.

CONTENTS

ACKNOWLEDGMENTS

I'd like to thank all the mentors whom I've had the opportunity to train with; you all have not only inspired, but have reached out to me in the times when I needed someone to lean on.

Also, far be it from me to think that the I could ever outshine any of the people whom I have worked with; if it weren't for the reflection of your successes, I'd have no shine at all.

Special thanks to Robert G. Allen, Jack Canfield, Deepak Chopra, Stephen Covey, T. Harv Eker, Mark Victor Hansen, Gay Hendricks, Adam Markel, Bob Proctor, Tony Robbins, Jim Rohn, Brian Tracy as well as so many others who have been influential and supported me along my life's journey.

Thank you to all my teachers and my students who teach me more than they know.

.

1

ARE YOU READY TO
LIVE YOUR BEST LIFE EVER?

I love my life so much… If I were to write a book about my life it would be nearly impossible because it would take so many books. I do refer to segments of my life when I write, so I write… and reveal stories, if appropriate and applicable.

Sometimes life goes the way I expect, other times I am surprised and shocked. I find that my life's journey is accompanied by joyous tears of gratitude and sometimes sadness making me love it even more.

Onlookers who love and care about me express deep concern when witnessing my experience facing life events that would appear to be insurmountable for someone else. They might try to console or counsel me, encouraging me to consider living a life more mediocre.

Mediocrity is not an option in my life. I am enjoying living my life full on and all in. Granted, this leaves me more vulnerable to disappointment or heartache but it also means that I enjoy and achieve more than someone afraid of taking the risk of living a wildly fulfilling life.

Life is like Walt Disney World. Some people are content looking at the view from their Orlando hotel with a WDW-facing view, that's good enough for them. Others might enjoy getting a day pass ticket, actually go in, buy some food and souvenirs, walk around, take some pictures and buy a tee-shirt to prove they've been there. Then, there are the adventurers who have to do it all.

I'm the adventurer who wants to feel the thrill of the ride, wondering for a moment if my next breath will be my last, to feel the exhilaration that comes from discovering that the ride continues. "Whew, made it past that," just to be surprised by what comes next. And don't forget, I want to be crying my eyes out to Jiminy Cricket and the Wishes fireworks show at the Magic Kingdom before I call it a night.

In my humble opinion,

Life is either a daring adventure or nothing

I am living my life as though I had a chance to select it from the universe's largest catalogs of life, like picking a movie from all the movies ever made, and after reading the synopsis for this one I said, "That's the one," and booyah, did I get my money's worth!

I realize that this approach to living a life where anything is possible may be too much for most people to handle, and that's okay. I don't judge, and honor your life's journey and your choice to live it out any way that brings you the most satisfaction, especially if you're loving your life as much as I'm loving mine.

For me and my life, I'm lovin' every minute of it. If you are not...

Well, maybe you just wanted to breeze through life without any surprises, or maybe you wanted to know what it would be like to live a life full of fear with impending suffering and danger... and if you are, consider this:

Is it possible that you chose to live a life that started out with lots of challenges only to make the happy ending that much more amazing?

Consider starting the most amazing part of your life today.

How much better does it get?

Well, it gets so much better than you could ever know, because not only is anything possible, but everything is.

I've spent most of my life in the personal and professional growth industry, surrounding myself with clients and mentors who are striving to be on the leading edge or have a burning desire to help make the world a better place. I have been blessed to work with some of the best minds in the mind sciences.

One common theme that runs throughout the waves of thought that permeate the sea of higher consciousness, is the belief that, "anything is possible."

Under normal circumstances, people are programmed to doubt their own sense of value – even though they came to this planet with a unique set of skills, abilities and unique message to share with the local community or the world – feeling as though they were not qualified to be a worthy messenger.

Usually, when I begin working with someone they are already on the path of achieving their highest and best or at the very least they have knowingness that their life is beckoning them to a higher calling and sense of fulfilled purpose.

Personal performance coaches start with the tenant of getting the client to a baseline understanding that there is ample well-documented, verifiable proof of things once thought to be impossible became possible starting with the thought that anything is possible.

This is not a new concept, as even New Testament's Jesus proclaims that all things are possible for he who believes (Mark 9:23) and many have gone on since to spread these words with different themes attached to it for clarity in certain situations, such as:

"If you believe in yourself anything is possible" or "Impossible only means that you haven't found the solution yet." A scientist-and-engineer friend of mine (referring to a quote by Henry Ford) says, "Anything is possible, with enough time and money."

Celebrities have chimed in with their varied view about anything being possible:

"With self-discipline, most anything is possible." ~ Theodore Roosevelt

"The best scientist is open to experience and begins with romance – the idea that anything is possible." ~ Ray Bradbury

"Nothing is impossible. The word itself says 'I'm possible'." ~ *Audrey*
Hepburn

"If you lead with passion anything is possible." ~ *Paula Abdul*

"Once you chose hope, anything is possible." ~ *Christopher Reeve*

"Anything is possible, if you've got enough nerve." ~ *J.K. Rowling*

"When doubt is banished, abundance flourishes and anything is possible." ~ *Wayne Dyer*

Even when Alice in Wonderland says, "This is impossible." The Mad Hatter counters with, "Only if you believe it is."

All this to say, anything that has ever been conceived, discovered or achieved was birthed in the thought that anything (currently believed to be impossible) is indeed possible – and someone believed it with enough fortitude – and had undertaken the task of making it so.

Napoleon Hill said, "Whatever the mind can conceive and believe, it can achieve."

We believe that anyone – yes, even you – have everything that you need to bring this thing to pass; and for some of us, it is our mission in life to support the efforts of an inspired individual to achieve the impossible.

But wait! There's more!

Believing that anything is possible is only the beginning. Yes, it can get you from here to there and beyond.

There is a superior concept that lies ahead in the horizon, that once it is truly grasped, changes everything and the belief that all things are possible begins to fade as one begins to understand:

Everything Is

I'll let you ponder that one…

Every moment of every day someone wakes up from the sleepwalking daily routine we call life, and in that moment of clarity recognizes that something's not right.

Remember being asked, "What do you want to be when you grow up," when you were a youngster?

Ever notice how your answer changed as you grew older? Chances are, when you were younger, you were more optimistic and fanciful about your future… (Most likely) by the time you were ready to finish school, your dreams had been reduced to feeling as though the only hope in life for a glimmer of happiness was to:

GO TO COLLEGE TO
GET A GOOD JOB
END OF STORY.

Did you know when you were born, your life had meaning? You came into being with a message and a special purpose. As you began to communicate and articulate your thoughts, you doubtless knew what your message would be and what your life's purpose was.

In your younger years, you would do things that were congruent with your message and purpose and it would amaze those who witnessed you exercising your gifts, but as you aged the same people who encouraged you in your youth by saying, "That's amazing," were now chanting, "but you need to forget all that and think about getting a good job."

Slowly, but surely, your mission (your message and purpose) was quashed (regarded as fanciful childlike dreams that would never come true) as you were groomed to be nothing more than a cog in the machine of life. You felt like denying your true calling was a good thing, in an effort to find a place to fit in society and survive with little impact, as the inner voices that were beckoning you to fulfill your mission faded away and were lulled to sleep.

The Awakening

Then, at some point in life, there is an awakening. That moment when you look in the mirror and say,

WHO AM I?
HOW DID I GET HERE?

Surveying your surroundings of the life you've succumbed to, you say to yourself,

THERE MUST BE MORE TO MY LIFE THAN THIS.

This is the heart (which always holds the key to your highest and best) breaking through to communicate with your brain (which has been reprogrammed to protect you from your heart). Your heart will make the best of the life you allow, but true fulfillment and heart-felt satisfaction can only be realized when you are living in harmony with your mission, until then, there will always be a degree of dissatisfaction or longing for something more.

This awareness (even if in brief moments of clarity) will alert your consciousness that something's got to change. Then you have to make a choice:

Recoil or Reposition

You can second-guess, let the haunting voices of the nay Sayers overcome you or talk yourself out of taking action, recoil and continue to block yourself from you mission, or you can begin to reposition yourself for something new, readying yourself to take action and find the answer to

WHAT IS MY MISSION?
HOW DO I START?

It is at this point in the awakening process that people are attracted to me (and others in similar fields) for assistance in finding purpose, increased quality of life (including health and wealth) and help achieving your highest and best.

The more open you are, the less assistance you need; you don't need anyone's help, if you can remember back to your childhood – or already have an intuitive knowing – recalling your message and purpose. Then, you can...

Take Action

You owe it to yourself to take action every day – no matter how small – to engage your purpose, to share your message. As you begin to embrace who you truly are (not the mediocrity society has come to expect from you) you will find, see and make new opportunities to exercise your gifts and talents to maximize your mission.

Resonate and Celebrate

This is the satisfaction that I receive in my line of work, to be there in the moment, to celebrate with a client who is resonating with their true sense of empowerment in aligning their lives with their calling. ***How much better does it get?***

Of course, this is MY calling, helping people achieve their highest and best, so little could be so thrilling. (See, it affects me the same way.)

Congratulations!
Your YOU is coming through

If you're reading these words, you're either awake or in the process of awakening…

How exciting!
So happy for you
Great things are coming your way…

Maybe it's time you started singing your song.

I grew up around music and was constantly singing to the radio or vinyl recordings as a youngster. From 1974 to 1994 I was chronicling my life's journey in song. I started playing professionally in nightclubs at a very early age. Overhearing instructions by the nightclub owners, "You can only play songs that are BMI licensed," and seeing musicians being sued over music rights in the news put the fear of the music industry in me.

So, I thought the only way not to get sued for playing music, was to write my own songs (originally fear-based songwriting). As I embraced the process, these songs became my musical scrapbook, the soundtrack for the stories spanning twenty years of my life.

I always knew – even as a young child – that I had a message and a mission, and though it has taken many forms along the way, I have stayed active and true to my life's calling; and sometimes my message is sung. I never claimed to be a proficient singer or songwriter, only a man with a message burning inside, aching to get out in any way possible and I didn't let my ability (or lack of ability) keep me from singing my song.

You came to this planet with a song to sing. What is your message, your song? Your message/song is unique to you. No one can tell you what song you should sing because it is your song, and your song alone.

Managerial structures that govern the publicly accepted views revered by our earth's inhabitants would like you to think it is okay to sing a song, as long as it isn't too radical or upsets the status quo. Plus, just like anything else, only individuals "qualified" should participate in such activities.

This underlying philosophy will keep most of the individual song-singers in check and when you're trying to find or sing your song, you may start to interrupt yourself due to doubt propagated by the idea that

- I'm not good enough
- I'm not educated enough
- I'm not strong enough
- I'm not qualified enough
- I'm not a good singer
- I'm not from a musical family
- I'm afraid to sing in front of people

And any other barrage of self-doubt and excuses to keep you from singing your song. If you don't sing, they win; your message is stifled, your candle light is snuffed out and the community at large suffers.

Believe me, there is someone who needs to hear your song. I have countless stories of people who were moved by particular songs that I've written and/or performed... some have truly amazed me. Because even though I wrote a song with a specific subject matter or purpose, the listener was moved in an impactful manner; and when they explain to me how the song spoke to them, I can't even imagine how they could have interpreted the subject in such a way.

Obedient sharing will bless others in ways you could never expect

It's like being obedient to sharing your message, will bless others in ways you could never expect.

If someone is drawn to you, they may need to hear your song... If you are singing, the universe will bring people to you to hear your song. It may be only one person, a small group of folks or thousands of people; it doesn't matter.

What matters is that you sing your song. If you're ready to live your best life ever, sing.

2

DO YOU WANT TO MAKE
THE WORLD A BETTER PLACE?

There are so many ways to segment peoples of the world; by race, by income level, education, political view, genetics, and sociological traditions, whatever… For me, it comes down to core motivation by answering the question, "Do you want to make the world a better place?"

It's not the end-all be-all qualification, but it's an important part of establishing a person's character.

Some of you might think this is a simple yes or no question, right? Well, it turns out its terribly complicated. I've always held to this tenet like the Holy Grail, because the idea is a driving force throughout my whole life. I often ask myself, "What can I do today – or in this moment – to make the world a better place?" even if only in some small way.

Having this particular mindset has me on the lookout for others who are motivated in the same way, because couldn't we all impact the world in a massive way for raising love, understanding, consciousness or global peace if we could join together?

So, I routinely ask the question, "Do you want to make the world a better place?" A glowing 90 percent of people answer, "Yes." Wa-hoo! I've found a soul-brother or soul-sister!

Then, to qualify we are sharing common ground, I ask, "What does that mean to you?"

This is where it all starts to fall apart. My joyous enthusiasm starts to wane, as they scrunch their nose, squint, tuck their chin and ask, "What?"

If they can provide me with an intellectually sound reply, I challenge them with, "What did you do today to make the world a better place?"

I am surprised how complicated such a simple question could be. The problem appears to be that we – all of us – have our own interpretation of the question, "Do you want to make the world a better place?" And if we are at all concerned about making the world a better place, each of us has a different idea about what that might look like.

Kind'a like my, "What would you do with 20 million dollars?" question.

It appears the question is misinterpreted or lost in translation, because when I ask someone, "Do you want to make the world a better place?" the question they answer is:

"Do you want everyone in the world to think, act, believe and be like you?"

Which (I'm disappointed to say) is not the question.

And I'm as guilty of it as anyone. When I ask the question, it is from my individual point of view. To me the question infers random acts of kindness, spreading love and compassion, personal, emotional and spiritual growth, tolerance for all peoples, responsible care and tending of our planet, and more along this trend of thought.

Even though from my perspective my inference was full of intention and clarity, the person to whom I had proposed the question possesses an entirely different perspective and agenda.

Even you; if you would like to see the world a better place, you might have a completely different idea, like:

(List of other ideas deleted prior to publishing, due to my own ignorance)

I am humbled and humiliated by this rant, now.

I found myself listing the myriad of ideas that others had answered the question with that were not congruent with my own and found myself in judgment. Ranting... (Where's the tolerance in that?) participating in the problem myself.

I am the hypocrite, the problem. I am what's wrong with the world.

Regrettably, those things I despise still reside within me... It is an ongoing process...

Forgive me.

So, What Do You Think?

What you think, say and believe about yourself defines who you are. Thoughts and words are so very powerful, that if you could truly grasp the power they wield, you would not use them so haphazardly. Certainly they can be powerful weapons when discharged against others, more powerful than a loaded gun, but what about when you turn those loaded weapons and aim them at yourself?

Think about these powerful weapons rolling around in your head; what do you allow to occupy this sacred space. There is no more private or intimate space besides your mind – which, by the way, is hardwired to your heart – where your deepest thoughts, dreams, desires, fears and joy resides. You, yes you, have control over what proliferates the confines of your mind and heart. You.

You cannot blame life, life circumstance, any belief system, person, place, parent or thing for what thoughts you allow to persist in your thoughts.

Why must you take control of your thoughts? Because they are so powerful, they manifest in you and attract more of what you think about, causing a great tidal wave of whatever it is you're thinking about to head your way.

What you're thinking about yourself is who you become

If you have self-image thoughts or self-talk that may not be in your best interest, such as being disappointed in yourself in some way, then you are certainly destined to become the very thoughts that haunt you. Alternatively, the more positive thoughts you engage in about yourself, the more positive the person you are. It's really that simple.

If you think, "I'm not good enough," then you are not (or you might be good enough at first blush, but if you continue to entertain the thought that you are not good enough, then it will not be long before you are unworthy of much at all).

Your other negative thoughts about yourself follow suit:

- I can't do it
- I have the worst luck
- I'm such a loser
- I'm not worthy
- No one loves me, or alternatively, nobody cares
- I hate "my" (or "it, when I") _____ (fill in the blank)

It is in your best interest to me mindful of how and what you think about because those negative thoughts will steal any hope of having good thoughts, especially about yourself.

If a negative thought is a weapon that steals, then a positive thought is the cure that heals.

Trade Negative for Positive

If you're having negative thoughts about yourself, all you have to do is to catch yourself thinking the thought – stop – and rephrase the thought as positive self-talk in its opposite. So, I can't do it becomes, I can do it. I have the worst luck becomes, I have the best luck, etc…

Want to supercharge your transformation, just ramp it up with an immensely positive reframe, like, "I can do it amazingly, better than most people!" Or, "I have the most amazing luck, I always win!"

Why? Because what you think comes to pass. Use these powerful tools not to tear yourself down but to build yourself up, because you are so amazing!

What you're thinking about everything else grows and becomes more powerful

Here are those powerful thoughts at work again, this time affecting the world around you. If you're thinking about tortured souls, people, animals you not only attract more of these things to your awareness, but your thoughts create more of it in the world.

Yes, by focusing on the injustices, crimes, disasters and lack (of anything) you actually help to create more of it.

Please, try to stop thinking about bad things, because it only creates more bad things.

What can you do?

Think about the opposite good things, the solutions... and if you're as amazing as I think you are, start not only thinking but talking to others about the amazing answers that are unfolding, maybe take action. Write a letter to the editor, make a blog post, support or start a movement for good.

By taking a positive approach – and focusing on positive solutions – you become a powerful healing force, creating and making the world a better place.

Think and be what you want to see

And it is so

Then there comes a time in your life when you look in the mirror and ask yourself, "Is this all there is?"

And you might just find as you contemplate the meaning and quality of your life you've allowed yourself to accept. At some point, you may feel incongruency with accepting a life that is mediocre at best and you begin to consider you deserve the best and you will no longer resign yourself to living a mediocre life.

You draw the line in the sand – it stops here – you know your worth and never settle for less.

Society has programmed us to find comfort in mediocrity, to never expect too much from life, commercial products or services, or other people (even those closest to us) for that matter. These low expectations have lulled us into a basic state of trance where complacency is not only acceptable but begins to feel safe, if not good. And for the most part, it's an effective method of controlling the masses with the least amount of effort, if we can all stay in the haze of confusion feeling as though we're all in the same soup; until you're hit with those brief moments when the state breaks down.

Don't worry. You are surrounded by enough hypnotic stimuli to pull you back into the trance state no matter where you are. If you're looking at yourself in the mirror, you notice your hair, clothes, other items behind you… If you're walking or traveling, there's architecture, signage, cars, other people wearing different apparel… If you're in the wilderness, there's the sound of crickets, birds, flora and fauna to focus upon… There are the everyday concerns of life firing synapses in your brain, or your cell phone begs for your attention… and all of these are triggers that snap you back into your state of unconscious consciousness.

When you shift back into the comfortably numb soup you think, "I'm okay enough," as you get what you settle for and you've resigned yourself to being okay with that, too. And there's nothing wrong with that.

Overcoming Mediocrity

Then there are those who for whatever reason, resist returning to the state immediately, prolonging that moment of clarity. If you're one of these people, the time may have come for you to evolve into a grander version of yourself.

You focus intensely on the inconsistencies of mediocrity and vow to never settle for less. With your undivided attention, you pledge to expect more, give, live and love more, perform better with higher efficiency and increase your quality of life to achieve your personal best.

Personal Best

As you separate yourself from the fog of acceptable compliance you begin to explore the expansiveness of all this life has to offer. Armed with your new sense of clarity you're beginning to see things are not always as they seem. Your awareness is expanding as you start to take on individual characteristics that are uniquely you as you not only dare to be different but begin to transform and evolve into the new you, affecting every cell of your body and reprogramming your DNA.

All the while you're attracting and acquiring new skills and abilities (some you were born with) as you explore this emerging frontier being more pliable, open and give it all you got so as not to hinder your expansion and accelerate peak flow.

To be different you refuse to accept mediocrity and never settle for less than your best as you give it all you've got to only settle for the best from this point forward because you deserve the best. You know that now.

And for those who continue on their path accepting mediocrity, you realize we're all just doing the best we can with what we have. When their time comes (and it will) they will realize they don't have to continually settle for less than the very best this life has to offer. You do not focus on the evolution of others, while you allow them the time and space to find their own way with love and acceptance.

It's all on you as you begin to cycle and recycle through your ever emerging **new personal best**.

Thankfully, I find myself mostly surrounded by like-minded people throughout my day who are able to keep me "in check" when it comes to managing my vibration.

As much as I try to stay focused in high frequencies, every once and a while I slip into lower vibrations.

Yesterday, on two different occasions, I began to rant...

If you know me, you know I don't succumb to this negative vibration very often as I am a very tolerant person. Nonetheless, there I was complaining about this (medications that make us sick) and going off about that (politics).

Luckily, someone was listening in who was able to bring my attitude to my awareness, just by saying, "I don't usually hear you go off, like that."

It was as if those were the magic words triggering my being knocked out of a trance.

I was, like, "You're right. How did I get all riled up, like that?"

So, I retraced my steps.

It shouldn't have surprised me that the catalyst for engaging my lower self was media – not via the radio or TV, mind you – sources I sought out myself (or was force-fed). The culprits: Google and Facebook.

It's the same ol' thing: You're looking for one thing, and you get distracted by a bazillion other things tugging at your lower emotional states. If you give in, this lowers your vibration which begins to attract other influences and circumstances to match your new level of vibration. If left unchecked for long, the next thing you know, you're feeling bad and you're bombarded with a downward spiral of more negative thoughts, attracting more negative people, circumstances and bad luck.

This is one of the basics of the Law of Attraction (LOA).

I am so grateful that someone who knew me well enough was able to get my attention mid-rant (twice in the same day), else the rest of my day might have spun out of control. Especially, since this was early on in the day. I mean, how effective can I be in helping people achieve their highest and best, if I'm unable to maintain my own state of peak performance?

Left unchecked, I would have stayed distracted by the media and become a distraction, myself, distracting anyone around me and potentially reducing their vibration also.

Granted, I cannot place blame solely on Google and Facebook. Clearly, I was already predisposed to allowing the disruption of the negative information that triggered me, like a Manchurian agent. There have been many occasions, when I have been exposed to the same type of information, and was able to breeze by it without a hitch. But yesterday, they got me and I feel somewhat ashamed of myself for falling for it.

I am usually more aware of my state of mind and presence, yet, there I was, caught off-guard and up in the negative whirlpool.

I know better than this.

I'm fairly adept at taking responsibility for maintaining my personal vibration. I couldn't help but think about others, who may not even be aware of how important vibration is to sustaining a high quality of life, how much more difficult for them must it be to resist the barrage of negative vibration onslaught of information?

It's no wonder so many people think life sucks.

How do you raise your vibration?

3

THIS IS HOW YOU DO IT

Aren't we all just trying to get through this life a little better than the day before?

You don't have to be the most charismatic, influential, famous or rich person on planet earth but just being a little better, doing something – anything – to bring you closer to what you want or make the world a better place… that's a day worth living in a life well-lived.

"One day at a time" is not just a recurring mantra of Alcoholics Anonymous or the (trademarked) television show starring Bonnie Franklin. Mackenzie Phillips and Valerie Bertinelli… No, it is the baseline of each of us traversing our own individual journeys along our own life path.

How you make it through each day is not to be compared to anyone else's day. Your life is for you, and you alone; this is not a competition.

I will admit, sometimes it's hard to make it through a day at all. And as I look around surveying my people, the people I've known, been fond of or have loved... I can't help but notice they have all but given up (and some of them have "thrown in the towel" even taken their own lives).

I have been blessed with the most amazing life. I wake up each day wondering

What will happen today?

Mostly, it's with the anticipation of a child waking up to Christmas morning... though sometimes there are the darkest of mornings when I ask, "What will happen today?" feeling as though my heart cannot beat one more time or it's too hard to take one more breath... but I do. And one breath leads to the next and the next comes a little easier and I find myself amidst yet another day.

Finding yourself amidst a day contains a challenge. A challenge not just to make it one more day, but to make this day a little better than the day before.

I am so grateful that making a day better than the day before isn't always about me. Certainly, I am the key player in my life, but making someone else's day a little better might just be the bright spot in my day. When I feel as though I have nothing left for me, I find blessing in the ability to encourage someone else's day.

A simple smile, compliment or friendly wave might be all someone needs to encourage them to take one more step, making it closer to achieving one more day.

If I can encourage one person to keep striving to live a good life and to help others reach out to someone else in the same manner... This kind of viral love and compassion – *even in the smallest doses* – can help to ultimately make the world a better place.

And all it took was to take another breath, take another step and to show a little kindness.

In a world that's off-the-hook with crazy insanity that can be so overwhelming that who of us has not considered that we might be better off somewhere (anywhere) else?

Yet, in this crazy world

You are the light

If even the smallest light, together we bring even more light to others… and the world.

Not only can you make a difference in this world

You are the difference

"Vive la difference!"

You make life worth living.

To embark upon this journey the onus is on us to plug in and turn on.

Whether in personal or professional life, you excel at certain things because the activities you enjoy maintain a certain vibration. The activity's vibration matches a vibration within you and as sports professionals say, you are "in the zone."

When you are in the zone you sort of get lost in the activity. The resonance is such a perfect match to your inner core that it appears to create an effortless vortex and time just fades away as you are immersed in the activity.

This kind of focused attention maximizes your performance and while it feels good to get lost in this particular task, you might consider finding methods to channel it into other portions of life to benefit not only yourself but the community at large.

When you plug into this energy vibration you turn on your pleasure centers and expand your mind's concentration as you engage in this activity, so finding a method to plug in can affect all areas of your life and increase productivity.

Also note when you plug in and turn on your zone vibration it not only lights up your brain's processing centers but it simultaneously promotes emotional stability by naturally reducing cortisol (the stress hormone) relieving anxiety, depression and the tendency to feel frustrated or irritated.

Plugging in and turning on for a structured 20 minutes per day can optimize you brain's chemistry and enhance your personal performance. Think about structuring a break in the middle of the day, or when you're approaching burnout, unplug from the chaos and plug into the zone for twenty minutes.

When you emerge from your trance of focused concentration following your 20 minute charge, the vibration carries over into the task at hand. You now have an increased clarity and ability to more effectively deal with issues and tasks that were difficult prior to plugging into the zone. The zone vibration will fade commensurate with the more challenging the task at hand might be, but your heightened sense of awareness at the outset may be enough for you to more easily push through the process of dealing with a less than desirable task.

Your freshly recharged state improves mental and physical acuity while enhancing your ability to create offensive strategies rather than being on the defensive. You are calmer and experience a heightened capacity for deescalating potentially stressful circumstances.

Spending time in your vibrational zone also promotes creativity, opening up your subconscious flow to make new connections for problem-solving, looking at things from an alternative perspective leading to inspiration and better creative expression.

Look for cues throughout your day, when you feel a shortage of coping skills or are having feelings of frustration, irritation or feeling anger rearing its ugly head. Try to create an opportunity to take a 20 minute break to plug in and turn on in these moments. Also note the time of day you are having these feelings. You may find scheduling a personal zoning session for that time of day hugely beneficial.

By plugging in and turning on to charge your vibrational inner powerhouse, you not only increase your personal performance but you also enjoy reduction in fatigue and a greater sense of being more effectively present in the moment, with an increased ability to tackle difficult tasks and challenges.

How long does it take to get from where you are to where you want to be?

They say the best things in life are worth waiting for, and they usually follow up with examples of wine, especially red wines get more spectacular tasting and oxidant-rich with age, as is the case with whiskey which becomes smoother also. Then there is the cheese when aged to perfection has increased levels of vitamins and probiotics. More foods that are enhanced by age include tea, balsamic vinegar and pickles.

Other things get more valuable with age, like our homes and alternative investments (even if we were unable to preserve them through tough times, they do – or have – increased in value over time). Antiques also continue to rise in value over time.

Then there is YOU

Yes, you. As you continue to age you get so much better in so many ways. While some of the things that you once took for granted in your youth may be fading away, the you that is emerging, like the butterfly from the cocoon, is a much grander version of you than ever existed before.

In fact, the things you were greatly concerned about in your youth are increasingly less important. Things like being selfishly obsessed with your body image (you are getting more comfortable with the idea that there is no need to maintain your high school appearance), your smile and countenance take on a new sparkle accented by lines chronicling a life well-lived as you embrace the comfort and wisdom of your years.

Your new, more seasoned and transformed self begins to materialize as friendships strengthen and family bonds become cemented. The concerns of your youth fade as you become more tolerant and empathetic as your perception shifts and you see more and more from a wider and wiser perspective.

You are more able to embrace a peaceful state of mind and enjoy less stress because you are more likely to forgive than hold a grudge or judge someone else. Now you have come to the understanding that we're all just doing the best we can with what we have. In fact most negative emotions are falling by the wayside as you continue to see the folly of holding tightly such things in your youth.

As you embrace this new heightened sense of awareness, you realize your expertise achieving new heights as many of the tasks that took thought and concentration can now be performed with unconscious competence or simple muscle memory.

Your ability to make sound decisions are growing and you find it easier to maintain balance in all things such as your work and play, while adding greater value to the community at large. Now you can enjoy greater degrees of happiness than you might have ever allowed yourself to enjoy before.

And while technology enables you to enjoy all these things even more,

The Greatest of These is Love

You have a greater capacity for love, to love and be loved. Appreciation, acceptance and love of yourself flows outward to family, friends, mankind, fauna, flora, the earth and your beloved.

This is an extraordinary opportunity for you and me – and those, like us – who are in search of that perfect person with whom to grow old and enjoy these golden years in each other's presence.

I look forward to this next incarnation of love to be my highest and best experience, though finding my soul mate can be a daunting, time-consuming task, I gladly accept the challenge in an effort to taste the subtle, flavorful nuances of its fruit when the time is right.

If all the best things in life take time, this appears to be taking the most time of all things that have gone before, and so worth the wait. Because the best life is awaiting us, and we both know that to rush this most important decision – about whom we will spend the rest of our life with – may well be the greatest decision of all.

For it is not just our lives we take into consideration, but the lives of our families and being able to better serve our communities for a better world to come throughout the remainder of our lives.

So much anticipatory love, while I remain awaiting your appearance with open arms because you are worth waiting for, my love.

4

WE INTERRUPT THIS PROGRAM

You are on the path of personal growth and enlightenment. You are making excellent strives as your heart and mind begin to open more and more to the possibilities as your consciousness expands...

There exists a level of mass consciousness that permeates the inhabitants of the earth. How – or for what reason – these ideas and concepts are nurtured and promoted as they continue to proliferate is a subject for debate, or you can just relax and realize it simply is what it is.

Just when you have inkling that there may be more, life will cause another interruption: misunderstandings (carrying heavy emotional impact), natural disasters, political unrest and polarity, inhumane actions, breaches of security, a terrorist attack, a disfiguring or fatal disease outbreak, growing rates of depression, suicide, wars and rumors of wars... a near endless supply of distractions designed to pull your mind out of the ethers and place your attention firmly back on terra firma.

Yet, in spite of the distractions, you – chosen one – you persist and press on to the new awakenings that lay ahead. So, here you are, growing and expanding beyond what might be considered prudent by the general population as well as other unseen forces who sense you are on the brink of a breakthrough.

Just when you're about to move to the next level of your evolution, you are abruptly interrupted

As you approach this brink, alarms begin to sound in unseen stations in, through and surrounding our communities that send waves of uncomfortable discord emerging within your neighboring family, loved ones and citizenry, signaling them to notice your growth and do whatever is necessary to save you from your impending demise.

There are many distractions and obstacles in place to prevent the masses from even considering a path of expanded consciousness. Many societal systems (the Internet) and media manipulations are effective distractions that keep most of us in a state of moderate fear. In most cases, this fear is all that is necessary to keep the sui generis from seeking higher truth.

But you have been called – and you answered the call – to maintain your conscious evolution without regard to a lifetime of programming and all of the tools and systems in place to keep you in-line with the managed mind of the general populace.

Meanwhile, you must be stopped. You are a threat to all belief systems put in place to control the peoples of the world. You will be disrespected, ridiculed, possibly the subject of intervention… anything to save you from taking a bite from the fruit of knowledge.

It is not uncommon for individuals on the path of personal growth and change to meet massive disapproval. People are (and the world is) threatened by you. People will hate you and want to want to drag you down to their level. It is the nature of the mob cult, but because of their numbers, they see themselves as "normal" and you as the black sheep that some believe must be saved (brought back into acceptable alignment with the masses) or (though more extreme) destroyed (for your own good, in an effort to save you from a fate worse than death).

Since the most prolific new thought leaders have short life spans (as they are assassinated, or – more recently – simply die prematurely of "natural causes") those of us on the path to enlightenment continue to progress and grow, though independently, subversively in an attempt to survive for the benefit of the greater good.

And as we continue to expand in numbers, power and consciousness, there is an growing love and light that is affecting our planet and all its inhabitants, with very little notice… and things are beginning to change.

Oh, you might not see it with the naked eye, but it is there – and you are part of it – for without you and the rest of us, it would not be possible.

Even though the media – and all the powers controlling this planet – would like you to think that we are in dire straits or on the brink of disaster (or the end of the world), there is a growing consciousness that will continue to guide our planet toward the entertaining miraculous and leading us to true happiness, fulfillment, satisfaction and peace.

And while you're taking the high road for a better world, don't be surprised to discover that things are not always as they seem.

Often the subject of debate, two people witness the same incident, a group of people share the same experience at the same time and place, scientists researching the same problems, political parties examine the same set of statistics, on and on it goes, and everyone comes to a different conclusion.

The financial backbone of our society, legal and otherwise, actually depends, is powered by, and thrives on people's inability to agree.

Everything that we witness, see, experience is fed into ourselves via our observatory senses, the data collected by our nervous system is interpreted by our mind – which we know is a collection of data collected over a lifetime – and our brain tries to make sense of it all, arriving at a personal conclusion.

So, really, it's no surprise that people see things differently, especially if Miss Interpretation is participating.

And that's not even addressing the idea of spin. Spin is a tactic used to manipulate the perceptions of people about a specific event, idea, topic or occurrence. The spin technique is wielded by media, politicians, salespeople, educators, lawyers, parents and friends (not to mention those with less than honorable intentions) in an attempt to persuade the perception of others. In fact, just about everyone who would have a sense of pride or comfort knowing that someone agreed with them about something. In this sense, most of us are guilty of attempting to impose our personal spin or opinion on others, because hanging out with like-minded people gives us a sense of belonging.

Christopher Nicholas Sarantakos, better known by the stage name Criss Angel hangs out in Las Vegas (one of my favorite towns), freaking people out by demonstrating that things aren't always what they seem better than anyone. Everything is explainable, once you know the secret. So, he can levitate – or appear to levitate – on an open street without the use of harnesses of wires. The question in my mind is, "Can anyone truly levitate."

I know people, in spiritual circles, who believe it is possible. Could a normal person (someone besides Criss Angel) levitate on a public street?

Criss understands better than anybody that perception influences everything we experience. More often than not, we have a choice to determine our individual conclusion, even if a master illusionist has stacked the deck in his favor.

Clearly, things are not always as they seem and this is the basis of many inspirational stories, like this story of two angles on a terrestrial stroll:

Two traveling angels stopped to spend the night in the home of a wealthy family. The family was rude and refused to let the angels stay in the mansion's guest room. Instead the angels were given a space in the cold basement. As they made their bed on the hard floor, the older angel saw a hole in the wall and repaired it. When the younger angel asked why, the older angel replied ..."Things aren't always what they seem."

The next night the pair came to rest at the house of a very poor, but very hospitable farmer and his wife. After sharing what little food they had the couple let the angels sleep in their bed where they could have a good night's rest. When the sun came up the next morning the angels found the farmer and his wife in tears. Their only cow, whose milk had been their sole income, lay dead in the field. The younger angel was infuriated and asked the older angel "how could you have let this happen!? The first man had everything, yet you helped him," she accused. "The second family had little but was willing to share everything, and you let their cow die."

"Things aren't always what they seem," the older angel replied. "When we stayed in the basement of the mansion, I noticed there was gold stored in that hole in the wall. Since the owner was so obsessed with greed and unwilling to share his good fortune, I sealed the wall so he wouldn't find it. Then last night as we slept in the farmers bed, the angel of death came for his wife. I gave her the cow instead. Things aren't always what they seem."

An inspirational story that depicts there could be more going on than what meets the eye.

Maybe the next time you quickly come to a conclusion about a certain person, place, thing, event or circumstance or someone tries to persuade you to think something, you might consider taking a moment to pause (breathe) and do some investigation on your own before drawing a premature conclusion.

Just some food for thought, as we all know – more often than not – things are not what they seem, at first.

How many times have you found yourself offended by the words and deeds of another person that may have been unwarranted? Even if you knew your feelings were likely unjust, still you found yourself filled with angst and fury and lashed out or made a rash decision based on the emotional whirlpool pulling you down to your lowest desperate state.
So you strike out, do or say something in your defense because in this emotional chaos, you can think of nothing more than self preservation at all costs.

You rationalize your thoughts and actions based on the truth you are able to extract from the all the data that you have access to. Using your perception you convert the results of your research and statistics to come to a cognitive conclusion justifying the torrential chaos you felt in that moment based on your interpretation.

This happens every day, and how can you blame anyone for perceiving everyday occurrences via their individual perception? You can't. Why? Because we can only determine that is really truth from within. Only we know what is true for us based on our own interpretation of the information available to us at the time.

In example, take a look at Jasmine and Darnell. They are in their early thirties, recently involved in a romantic courtship and things are going so very well. They are professing their love for each other and even talking about spending the rest of their lives together.

On their six month anniversary, Darnell makes reservations for a quaint bistro, picks up a card and a teddy bear with a heart on its tummy and presents them to Jasmine when he comes calling to pick her up for their scheduled date.

Jasmine greets him at the door enthusiastically. Darnell holds out the bear and card to Jasmine, as her countenance immediately shifts to contempt and anger. She throws the bear into the street, rips the card into pieces and throws the pieces at Darnell's face and kicks him off the porch while shouting disrespectful obscenities and slams the door as Darnell falls to the ground.

After driving away and pulling over to the side of the road, Darnell texts Jasmine, which does not go through, then tries to call to discover his number's already been blocked.

Looking for emotional support, the couple reaches out to their friends in an effort to cope with the ensuing chaos. Jasmine tells her friends that Darnell is a manipulative predator, nothing short of a rapist, while Darnell spins tales of Jasmine's severe mental disorders. Friends rally around the couple. Damages follow, some that are irreparable.

Knowing the details of Jasmine's struggle with her past doesn't justify her outburst and reaction to the otherwise innocuous display of affection. Issues she's been battling within since childhood predicted her response with high-precision accuracy. Likewise, Darnell's accusations of Jasmine's mental instability were based on triggers from his past.

From their perspective they are both telling stories based on the truth they believe, as real to them as gravity, yet things aren't always what they seem and neither of them have as much information as I have (purposely filtered) additionally I am certain there is much more information yet to be uncovered.

Jasmine would fare much better in the same circumstance today, because she has worked though many of the unresolved issues of her past and while she still tends to be quite impulsive, is training herself to pause (and count to three to herself) before responding, reacting or pressing "send" when she is feeling overwhelmed. This brief hesitation gives her just enough space to consider possibilities, ramifications and helps her to manage her truth and consequences.

Don't judge someone based on surface information because you may have no idea what lies beneath the surface. We all have lives consisting of a plethora of past experiences, beliefs and misinterpretations the sum of which has gotten us this far. After all, we're all doing the best we can with what we have. This is why we are cautioned to never judge a book by its cover.

If we are to have any faith in our ability to successfully share this planet with other inhabitants, we must find ways to stop dividing us one against the other, discover how to get along with each other and accept that we are all parts of the same soup, even though we all are so very different.

No one is blaming you or me for our perception or interpretation, because in heat of the moment it's all we have to determine what is truth as it influences how I feel about you, how you feel about me and how we feel about ourselves.

In fact, in all things perception is reality and subject to change pending accumulation of additional data.

Pausing in an effort to avoid making a rash decision or burning a bridge beyond repair like Jasmine does now, might be sound advice for all of us.

All you can do is to try not to judge or react too promptly, accept others for who they are and where they are at in their life's journey and discover how to make yourself happy with your life. A little tolerance goes a long way.

For me, I try to imagine what it must be like to the person who is reacting, put myself in their shoes and look for the love. While I haven't perfected this method because I too, can react in self-defense in the heat of the moment… but as immediately as possible look with empathy for love in the wings.

We're all in process, for if we weren't, we would not be. Let's make the best of it, without getting in our own way and blocking ourselves from all those things we deeply desire.

Why is it that just when I'm about to make a breakthrough, I clumsily do something to screw it up?

Does this ever happen to you?

You are faced with opportunity, a job, a promotion, a romantic relationship, an investment, a business opportunity, then just nonchalantly watch the whole thing go sideways based on your action – or inaction – that, when you look back on it, you KNEW nothing good would come from it?

Why do we do that?

Self-Sabotage

It's as if there is something inside us that makes us believe that we are not worthy of all the goodness this life has to offer and this underlying belief becomes a self-fulfilling prophesy. Then your mind can reassure itself with a resounding, "You see: I knew it was too good to be true."

I told you so

But isn't the truth of the matter that you were given this life and all it contains to have happiness, joy, fulfillment and the ability to achieve your highest and best?

If you could just wrap your head and your heart around it.

If not, you will continue to destroy every good thing that could potentially happen to you. This is a self-protection safety mechanism built-in to your subconscious, based on fear. The fear that something bad might happen, or you might be disappointed, because we all know

It Happened Before

At some point (or several points) in our lives (beginning in our youth) we had a hope, a dream or a projected outcome that did not come to pass and it broke our heart or spirit. It felt bad not to enjoy our expected result in the way we had hoped. We thought it would feel so good, felt like we were fortunate and somewhat worthy (or at least lucky) enough to be able to enjoy this one moment, only to watch it fall to pieces before our very eyes.

Danger – Danger – Danger

Our subconscious (in concert with our conscious mind) goes about the work of protecting our fragile feelings, setting up our life in such a way as to never be disappointed again, for we would be better off not to have any expectations, wealth, feelings, love, joy or happiness, than to take a chance and suffer loss.

To protect ourselves from feeling let down, or taking the risk of making the wrong decision we screw up every opportunity we are presented with in an effort to protect that fragile little child who lives within us – who secretly desires to have all these things – but would rather die than take a chance at truly enjoying anything… ever.

Low Expectations

It's as if keeping expectations so improbably low, and seeing destruction all around you does one thing. It proves that you are right and you can justify your pathetic state of mind because

Nothing Good Ever Happens

And all your observations seem to support your state of mind. Whether it happens to a friend, relative, stranger, innocent bystander or you see it on the news. Bad things happen to people all the time. It happens everywhere to everyone every day, and they're not alone. We're all in this boat together, "Life Sucks" for everyone 24 hours a day 7 days a week… and so it is.

Your resistance to allowing goodness into your life is the most effective way to protect yourself from disappointment because in this way you are sure never to have the expectation of anything better than achieving numb mediocrity… and that's better than putting one's self at risk of getting your feelings hurt.

Positive Thinking

You could live out the rest of your life this way, or you could experiment with happiness and joy just by exercising your imagination and thinking about something good. You don't have to make any huge commitments to change your life in any way, or battle with any inner demons lurking within. All you have to do is to dip your toe in the water to find some sense of feeling good.

You risk nothing by exercising your imagination. Try it. Close your eyes and think of a joyous thought (or moment) when you felt thoroughly happy. See it in your mind's eye and remember every detail of it, the colors, the smells, the lighting, the feel of it and smile.

See. You were happy and you did not die.

Maybe there's hope for you, yet.

Isn't Now the right time to start living a happy life?

Since you are a physiological representation of your vibrational energy. Note these important contributions to maintaining your personal frequency of vibration:

INTENTION
ACTIVITIES
FRIENDS

We are energetic composites of what is our own ideas about how we see ourselves or would like others to see us (intention), how we spend our time (the activities in which we engage) and the people with whom we associate with (who you hang with).

When we interface with other people, our energetic interaction will either influence the person with whom we are communicating positively or negatively. When you speak to someone do your words express life or death? When we communicate with others our words are charged with our own vibrational energy the result will either have a healing effect on the recipient or a harmful effect.

Realizing this puts an incredible amount of pressure on those of us who are on a constant and never-ending path of increased performance and personal growth. It means accepting responsibility for how our own energy, words, and method of communication affects those around us.

Intention

Everything begins with intention. I could only assume that your intention is to have a healthy, healing and positive impact on the lives of anyone with whom you are interacting.

Our intention affects the delivery of our message greatly. It influences our body language, voice inflection, choice of words and the general "feeling" that is felt by the recipient. Even if our words are carefully and cognizantly selected, if they are not consistent with our energetic field, the person you're trying to communicate will not be able to receive your intended message, for they will sense the incongruency and they will be more confused than receptive.

Taking a breath and a moment to set your intention and connecting with your heart before engaging in a conversation (or performance) can help to set the stage for a more effective experience.

Activities

How you spend your time sets the frequency for your personal energetic vibration. It doesn't take a rocket scientist to figure it out, either. You know how to evaluate what frequency you are tuned into by how you feel about a particular activity. Some of the activities that you engage in do not make you feel good, they send you reeling down the energetic vibration scale. How you feel is a clear indication of where you are on the scale.

How do you feel when you watch the news? How do you feel when you listen to a debate? How do you feel when you play a video game?

How do you feel when you hear (or participate in) gossip? Gossip, or talking behind someone's back disrespectfully, is an interesting energetic phenomenon. When you engage in gossip you engage in a negative energetic vibration that seeks out the subject of your conversation and sends harmful energy to him or her. Is that really something you want to do? Even if the recipient doesn't know you, they still feel your negative energy. (This is a scientific fact.)

On the other hand, how do you feel when you volunteer to feed the homeless? How do you feel when you hold a baby in your arms? Snuggle with your cat (or dog, etc...)? How do you feel when singing in the shower, taking a walk along the water, or watching a beautiful sunset?

In terms of your energetic vibration, you are what you do. That is to say, the activities that you participate in sets the tone (vibration) that permeates your life, fueling and determining the energy field surrounding you that affects everything else you do.

Friends

It is said that you will be the average of your best five friends, the five friends that you spend the most of your time with (which may not be your "best" friends, for you might have friends that you are closer to, but spend less time with).

So, who are the friends (or people) that you spend the most time with? What are they like? Are they the type of people that you aspire to be? What is their average energetic vibration?

Their energetic vibration will influence yours, and yours will tend to find a resonant vibration similar to their energetic average. So, if you aspire to maintain a higher vibration, it is advisable to spend more time with folks who maintain vibrations higher than yours. This will help raise your vibration.

The knowledge of all this and your ability to take responsibility for your vibration empowers you to keep on track in terms of achieving your highest and best.

And let's face it, without friends to share the good moments in life with, it reduces one's quality of life. And if you've taken the position of, "I don't need no stinking friends," then it is certain that you will not have any. If you ever find yourself in need of a friend (which happens from time to time) you will not have anyone to turn to when it would be beneficial to have someone you could lean on.

I'm not saying you have to have a hundred friends, although someone I work with has hundreds of friends – probably the most connected person I've ever met – and while he maintains genuine friendships with them, when he needs a friend for anything (personally or professionally) a simple text, email or phone call is all it takes for them jump at the opportunity to help him. A few friends, like four or five, who live in within a hundred miles or so would serve you well.

These should be special friends. That means they are compatible, share some of the same interests and passion as you, are integrous, trustworthy and you will have each other's back. It's not likely this will happen overnight but to remain open and willing to invite a few special people into your life would help to attract the right kind of people but don't expect your new friends to instantly materialize in front of you.

You have to put yourself in the right places to find friends who are the kind of people that would make good friends. You might even have to create opportunities to find friends. Consider joining an organization, creating your own club, networking event, regular themed meet up or meeting that will attract participants who are likely to share similar interests.

As you're attracting a core group of friends who will "have your back" and you theirs, keep in mind that you are not desperate, and do not try to force a friendship. If you're in the right place at the right time, a potential friendship will blossom naturally. Though you may need to make the first move (invite someone to coffee, etc.) be thoughtful enough not to seem aggressive while finding friends. Maintaining a genuine friendship is not hard work; they simply grow and mature without much effort.

Once you've met someone in public, you will need to move to a more private arena to build a relationship. True friendships are built off-line, not just during breaks at events. If you think you are too shy, you might want to practice putting yourself out there enough to create bonds with people you might like or learn to love if given the chance.

If you find a friend, or two, at a particular event or venue, it may be time to reach out to another group of people or to hang out with their other friends at other get-togethers to give you new opportunities to find potential friends that can grow into authentic relationships.

It is important to maintain a sense of community. You may find your regular circle of friends and family are not as supportive of your goals, dreams and desires – and may not even recognize a win for you as such, so – expecting them to celebrate with you would be confusing to them. But a group of like-minded individuals will "get you" and celebrate enthusiastically, helping to cement your new plateau, and encourage you to reach even farther on your quest to your highest and best.

These people could end up being your most trusted long term friends for life.

5

DEALING WITH RELATIONSHIPS

Idle words. Talk, talk, talk…

Notice how everyone loves to get the latest dish from you about what's up with whom? You like having their full attention to hear all the latest dirt. You keep your ear t the ground and are ready to serve up a fresh serving of dirty laundry with the compelling, "Word on the street is…"

You don't think twice about saying something about others behind their backs. Ever wonder what others think about you behind your back? Chances are, the very same people who love to hear you spin your attention-getting headlined yarns about the private lives of others, are wondering (and concerned) about what you are saying about them when they're not in your presence.

You may not realize, when you're reporting the latest gossip, what you're really communicating to your listening audience is, "I can't be trusted."

There is a deeper connection and level of communication that takes place between people who possess a high degree of trust between them. The gossiper is less likely to have this type of deep connection with another person, and if this level of communication does exist, it will likely deteriorate in the light of continued gossip as the once-deeply-connected individual recoils in fear; fear of betrayal, anticipating what you might report about him/her to others to garner attention and amusement.

If you are in the habit of spewing idle words when others are not present, you might consider doing just the opposite. When you are talking about someone and the details of their life, make certain that you are talking to the person who is the topic of your story. It really is that easy. If that person is not present, don't say it.

In business, management often struggles with the milieu of the rumor mill among the workforce, as it eats away at the fabric of productivity and breaks down an otherwise cohesive team network. Responsible businesses maintain a gossip-free zone, and when someone's story-telling is detected at the workplace, measures are taken to get the storyteller and the subject face-to-face, while reinforcing (or enforcing) the no gossip policy.

Being in the business of helping others puts me in a position to maintain a high level of confidence with my clients. They tell me their deepest, darkest secrets, hopes, desires and dreams. Over the course of my life's work, I've heard it all, and it is my responsibility to maintain confidentiality and respect the non-disclosure of the intimate details of their lives.

As fascinating as it might be to hear about someone else's dirty laundry, when someone has the propensity to go on and on about other people's life, more likely than not, I will turn the conversation around to the storyteller, with a, "Tell me how this affects your life," or, "Have you ever found yourself in a similar situation?" Or I might ponder out loud, "Hmm, I wonder what it must feel like to be in that person's shoes?" while shifting into, "Tell me about you…"

By disengaging in the activity of talking about others behind their backs, people will be less likely to consider you to be potentially toxic, begin to trust you more and you will be able to enjoy the benefit that comes from having deeper, more meaningful, connections with other people.

Burning Bridges

Sometimes, in relationships (business, personal or otherwise) it is necessary to burn the bridge that connects one person with another, so that there is little or no possibility of crossing over it again. Such is the case of those engaged in an abusive relationship or in the event that you are entangled with a psychopath.

In my work with individuals making their way through this life it is not uncommon for me to work with someone harboring deep regrets about a bridge-burning episode in life that was fueled by a temporary emotional state. Though the emotional state was temporary (and appeared more significant, even emergent, at the time) the resulting bridge destruction was permanent.

Many people in their last moments tell stories about their regrets about bridges burned beyond repair in their lives, the result of their own incendiary devices, that if ever given the opportunity of a do-over, they would have done it differently.

Working with people who are on their individual path of personal or spiritual growth, occasionally the subject of severed relationships – relationships dissolved with a life sentence and no possibility of parole – surface in the form of regret.

In doing the work of achieving one's highest and best, you never know who can be an asset to your growth or potential, the idea is to retain as many options in your life as possible. Think about the options in your life being represented as a deck of cards; shuffle the deck and you have 52 options. Now, shuffle the deck again, only this time pick a card – any card – and burn it. No problem, now you have 51 options. Repeat the process another 50 times and now you're down to your last card.

You no longer have the ability to shuffle or burn a card and you are left alone with no options.

People are the conduit connecting the events and opportunities traversing throughout our life. Making a habit of irrevocably severing connections with other people is counter-productive to say the least, because it limits your opportunities exponentially. When you burn a bridge between you and another person, it is likely to be noticed or affect someone else.

Do you think successful people with integrity are in the habit of burning bridges? Only if it is absolutely necessary and no other way can be found to circumvent the severance. Even so, care is taken to minimize the damages or potential extenuating ramifications. They painstakingly attempt to preserve and retain all the cards they have.

Yet, not all of us can conjure up the necessary fortitude to conduct all of our relationships with this level of social prowess, especially when emotions have the better of us. In the immediacy of the moment – feeling as though there is no other option but to fight or flee – burning the bridge seems like the best option at the time, in an effort to preserve one's self. It's as if, in that moment, you felt as though your life depended on the permanent separation.

With a few cards burned from your deck, you can still likely survive, but if you continue to burn cards the community at large sees this and begins to further reduce the number of opportunities otherwise available to you. The universe also matches your opportunities based on how you manage your cards.

If you're in the habit of saying (or thinking), "I'd rather be alone than…" Don't be surprised if you are rewarded with more alone time, or less quality time with others.

Mending Fences

On the bright side, bridges are rarely FUBAR (beyond repair). A little fence-mending can go a long way as you continue your life's journey. Though waiting for the other party to initiate the reconstruction is ill-advised. Remember, the universe is watching you and rewards you with what you give.

If you are more likely to reach out in forgiveness and not alienate others (unless it's absolutely necessary) then you can expect to receive more of the same.

Your future will be brighter, satisfying and you will enjoy more happiness, without the remorse that comes with extricating others.

Build a bridge

It can be as easy as saying, "How's it going?" This may be enough to bridge the gap. It needn't be a full on apology, "I'm sorry, I don't know what I was thinking," or, "I was just overwhelmed at the moment," and, "not thinking straight," or any combination thereof. But you might offer up such a response if challenged with, "I thought you hated me."

But in most cases, people are pretty much open and forgiving to others but we tend to make things more complicated in our mind's eye than is so in reality.

A little humility goes a long way, plus it puts you back in the driver's seat as you increase your opportunities and take back the power of your own heroism.

Maintaining relationships may not be your strong suit. I have worked with many clients who feel inept at dealing with other people due to the familial environments in which they were reared. They feel they face many roadblocks in life because they have a dysfunctional family.

An honest review of what is now the acceptable standard for family relationships is a far cry from the family dynamic of yesteryear. Are you happy with the way your family is?

It breaks my heart to see how far we've fallen, as there's little respect for the family unit in comparison and chances are, if you're a member of a family, you too have found yourself a member of a

Dysfunctional Family

By definition a dysfunctional family is a group of individuals related by blood, marriage, or living arrangements that experiences conflict on a fairly regular basis. I believe this defines every family, so there's nothing that unusual about being a member of a dysfunctional family, unless an abusive relationship threatens the family unit requiring intervention.

Even so, even "abusive relationships" can (and often are) exaggerated to effect a certain means to an end, without regard to the family member whose life may be sacrificed for the sake of his or her accuser, further exasperating the dysfunction of the family.

Nowadays, the expectation is that the whims of the individual outweighs the needs of the family, resulting in fractured families and broken homes causing more discord, especially when children and family suffer the consequences.

Unfortunately, the divorce industry and social services support the destruction of the family, and doing so, actually supports our government and the economy... but at what cost?

Children are now used as a weapon, and income is not a barrier in this, as it crosses all income levels and tax brackets, though lower income families are privy to legal prowess that would only be available to the wealthier families due to their low income level thanks to support from the Department of Social Services, Child Protective Services and the family court system.

Certainly, we need a system to protect children and families being abused, but our system is greatly flawed, because a parent can use the existing system as a powerful weapon, destroying the life of another (who may be undeserving) at little or cost to the accuser. All that is required is that the accuser be willing to exaggerate and lie to a counselor and possibly to a courtroom under oath. A small price to pay for someone to use – just the implied threat, or equivalent of – "Don't mess with me or I will ruin you forever."

Blended Families

You recognize these, they're like the Brady Bunch; two single parent families with children from a different parent, come together to create a blended family, melding the families into one (hopefully) cohesive unit. In most cases, blended families actually consist of a single mom trying to find love, with children, partnering with a single dad (non-custodial), strapped by extenuating circumstances, visitation with child support and legal issues of his own. Though, some blended families are able to prevail and create a healthy family environment, regardless of the challenges they face.

The results? Look at the prison system filled with the people who were the children raised in these dysfunctional families. Why? It really is a choice. You can choose to live respectful life or a disrespectful life. I know. I come from as dysfunctional a family as you might be able to imagine. I chose to live a respectable life, regardless of my family life, and I vowed that when I entered marriage with the right person, I would maintain a higher standard of familial love, respect and support than was available to me in my youth.

Family First

My approach to family is simply, "family first." For me, that means that if I am with you and you are with me, then my family is your family and your family is my family. I have a great deal of love for my family and I extend the same quality of love and affection for your family members as I do my own (reciprocity would be a reasonable expectation).

Such a heavy commitment to family doesn't garner much respect in today's society.

I hope to see a bright future for the United States and throughout the world realizing, supporting and sustaining the importance of family fueled by family love, tolerance and strength of family.

In the meantime,

For me and my family

We love and support each other

But what can you do, when you're doing the best you can regarding the relationships in life, and have been betrayed by someone you trusted?

You've put your trust in someone because you're an honest, open person. The trust that you felt for this person was at such a high level that you let your guard down, possibly were more transparent than you've ever been… and now, you've been betrayed. Right now, you can even recall a time when you've felt so bad like you've been punched in the stomach, had your throat slit, been beaten and thrown into a ditch and left for dead.

Betrayal comes in many shapes and sizes, so it's difficult to discern what to do next, but be aware, when you've been stabbed in the back (so to speak) by someone you've trusted and you have been betrayed, it is important to get your wits about you, make healthy choices and take appropriate action in an effort to not make things any worse than they are right now.

Friend Betrayal

When you've been betrayed by a friend it cuts deep, especially it was a best friend betrayal, because the closer you are to a person (as in the case of a best friend) the more vulnerable you have been. It's likely that you've shared sensitive information that you entrusted to your best friend and now you're regretting having opened up so transparently. When your best friend betrays you it's reasonable to feel a range of emotions including sad, hurt, fear and anger.

When a friend betrays you (any kind of friend) the degree of vulnerability normally adjusts to the relationship's level of trust accordingly. Your friend could be a co-worker who has regular access to other co-workers and friends complicating things further.

"I can't believe my friend betrayed me."

When friends betray you, you can feel as though you need to defend yourself, strike back, flee or withdraw from society altogether. Yet, you should refrain from doing these things, if you can, when you've been betrayed by friends.

Family Betrayal

There is no doubt that family betrayal will rock anyone's world. I mean, if you can't trust your family who can you trust? Your level of exposure to family members is exponential when compared to friends. Your family knows just about everything about you and could use this information against you.

When family betrays you, hopefully, you have a friend you can trust, or seeking out a coach or counselor to help you keep your head screwed on straight as your family makes you feel as though it's just you against the world. You need someone in your corner, who can help you empathetically when your family betrays you.

Love and Betrayal

The one person that you have been the most exposed to is your love interest. Your boyfriend/girlfriend, fiancé, husband or wife knows you more intimately than anyone and when you've been betrayed by a lover, if you've been truly in love with this person, all your emotions will be maximized.

Little hurts worse than being betrayed by someone you've opened up to completely and have shared intimacy with. Your heart feels as though it's been stabbed and left bleeding out as you ponder, "Why?"

How to Deal with Betrayal

When you're immersed in the pain of betrayal, it's difficult to think straight. A simple exercise can be found in the next chapter entitled, "Tap It Out," you can perform that will release the pain of being betrayed and will help you to approach the betrayal from a logical perspective. Once you've been able to remove the pain, you will find yourself thinking more clearly.

You can find some peace by not thinking of yourself as a victim and realize that the person who has betrayed your trust and faith is not an evil person. In most cases the one who has betrayed you is a victim of life circumstances which has made him or her strike out at others in this way.

You will find that it is not so much about you, as it is the pent up pain and frustration of an individual suffering from low self-esteem, self-loathing and a life of pain which causes them to act out in this manner.

If you're an empathetic person, as you begin to realize this, you may be inclined to reach out to the person who has betrayed you in an effort to help him or her. This would be ill-advised, as it is not your job to try to fix this person, and it could be very well that this person is not salvageable. Even if he/she were, your attempts are likely to cause you more undeserved pain and loss.

You're better off avoiding the excess drama and find ways to move on.

You can find more ways to deal with betrayal in my book: Trust Betrayal.

While we're addressing the subject of managing relationships and understanding we are all basically the same, there are those who would like to maintain our separateness, and they're doing a good job of keeping us polarized against each other.

"Me, me, me. Mine, mine, mine." It starts at a very early age, and if left to itself, this polarization and entitlement can expand and grow, like a cancer, infecting our society. You would think with 7.4 billion people on our planet, we should start to find ways to coexist with less conflict.

You might be able to recognize the adult signs of polarization and entitlement and choose to be part of the solution for a better world.

I am the victim

"You don't understand, I am the victim, here."

When you see yourself as the victim of some kind of abuse, mistreatment or lack of respect, you polarize yourself away from the subject (person, place or thing) that has "wronged" you and greatly reduce the ability to resolve the issue without conflict. You have drawn the proverbial line in the sand and declared war on the situation.

Any further conversation or negotiation from this point forward will be in the form of debate. You post up and ready yourself for battle and start building your case to establish your affirmative position while imposing your view of how you have been harmed or disrespected. You are ready to fight.

You don't know me

"You have no idea about who I am, or the life I've lived."

To assume that no one understands me, my plight or my perspective, implies that it makes a difference. Of course, it is actually impossible for m to actually see anything from your perspective – you might be able to give me clues – but it is simply not possible. All of us are completely unique. Though we may share some things in common, no person can truly see anything from anyone else's perspective (unless we can figure out how to do the Vulcan mind-meld) and at times, we all feel like a Stranger in a Strange Land.

Don't trust anyone

"I don't trust you. I don't trust anyone."

When I was young, I trusted people. If I've learned one thing in my life, it's that you can't trust anyone – I don't care who you are – I cannot, and will not, trust anyone ever again, as long as I live.

Everyone is out to get me

"People are always trying to find new ways to put me down."

Rarely does a day go by (or a moment, for that matter) that someone doesn't disrespect me, falsely accuse or belittle me. I am an adult, I have rights and I demand to be treated fairly.

Sense of entitlement

"You owe me. I demand to be taken care of."

Whether it is being respected, heard, vindicated or to exercise vengeance, my expression must win out and any and all resources available can be called upon to satisfy my basic needs, desires or initiatives.

The idea that everyone should be the same; treated the same, the world is somehow responsible for catering to your every need or whim and your knowledge of how to manipulate the system to get you what you want (for the most part) satisfies your basic need(s).

Stop Intolerance

If you want to live a full and free life, full of happiness and satisfaction (with a little disharmony thrown in for flavor and personal growth) you must stop polarizing yourself against others.

Once you hold fast to the idea that it's me versus them, you have created an impossible situation that feeds the victim mentality and breeds discord.

It is not until we can wrap our heads around the idea that we are more the same than we are different. Instead of demanding our differences be recognized and respected, realizing – we are all human beings, sharing what resources are available, each making our own way, doing the best we can with what we have – we are all the same, and I love and respect you as much as I'd like to be loved and respected.

Sure, we love those things that create our own uniqueness and celebrate our individuality among the rest of us. We all have the right to our own ideas, ideals, philosophies, beliefs and those characteristics that make us different, but to impose them on anyone else would be disrespectful. Can't we all just get along?

Tolerance suggests that we all have the inalienable right to think or believe whatever we want, as long as it doesn't interfere with anyone else's right to the same.

BARNEY SAID IT BEST:

I love you
You love me
We're a happy family

Until we can love and be loved – allowing each individual their right to their own perspective, without having to defend it – will we see true harmony in our society and/or the world.

So, here you are, taking the high road of love and sharing your ideas with others… then one day you decide to post a concept that is private, near and dear to your heart, with the purest of intentions on the Internet.

Within moments, you may realize that your openness backfired as you were attacked by hating Internet marauders.

Whenever you reach out to do good in the world, expect a backlash from ignorant people who just don't get it. Not only do they not get it, but they have declared war against you and everything that you stand for, and they will stop at nothing (while hiding behind the Internet) to try to embarrass, defame and humiliate you via the World Wide Web.

The first thing to remember is that these people are not innately evil in any way. For the most part, they are lonely and pathetic people with little to live for, who have likely been abused or otherwise victimized in their pasts. Lashing out to authentic, heart-centered people promoting a better life are easy prey, and belittling them, in some way makes them feel a little better (or a little less worse).

So, try not to take the cyber-bullying personal, when you've shared something intimately from your heart, then get viciously attacked by an Internet troll (hater) who does his best to hurt your feelings and break your spirit.

How to Deal with Haters

So, what to do when you're attacked via social media?

The best course of action is nothing. That's right, just ignoring it is the best course of action. Do not respond or try to defend yourself because that just adds fuel to the fire. Just accept it for what it is. A victimized person, who is hurting inside, who can think of nothing better to cope with their pain than to victimize someone else, and using a somewhat anonymous vehicle, like the Internet, is a perfect way for them to strike out, without much risk.

Then there are the people who care about you and know that your inattentions were pure, and resonate with your point of view. Your supporters might rally against the cyber-bullying, in an attempt to vindicate your good name.

It Could Be Worse

I know, I thought the same thing. A few years ago, when I was viciously attacked via social media online by a psychopath rallying sadistic Internet trolls to join in slinging hate and discord about me, some other social media users were influenced to join in on attacking me, because I had been targeted as an evil person.

Immediately, my friends began to defend me and respond to the insensitive posting of the haters. Even though my energy was greatly depleted (the attacks ensued due to the loss of my son in Afghanistan) I tried to quickly respond (privately if I could) to beg them not to respond, because just as I had expected the controversy began to turn into full on battle.

As people stopped defending me, the Internet trolls and cyberbullies went away looking for other prey to post inflammatory comments about, for there is no satisfaction for them in attacking someone who will not result in someone expressing their being hurt, upset or becoming argumentative. This left the psychopath to remain alone as the only person left standing who continued to try to defame me.

Apologies and support started to come my way, after a while, from people who had been misled by the psychopath and his temporary herd of minions, after they had discovered the truth of the matter and realizing that they had been duped.

Follow Your Heart

Speak your peace, share your heart and let nothing dissuade you from sharing your innermost desires for goodness, love and hope for a better, brighter world.

Do not defend, or strike back, just let it go, let it be and it will fade away or find somewhere else to go. No need to judge, criticize or poke fun at the haters, because they're situation is probably worse than you can imagine.

Just be aware that there are people out there who are hurting, and while it's true that "Haters are gonna hate," realize they, too, are doing the best they can with what they have.

Your true friends and followers will respect your integrity by seeing you continue to smile and wave through the positive responses and the bad.

Let it go, don't let it get to you… Keep singing your song.

6

THE BEST STORY EVER
STARTS NOW

The best story ever has yet to be written but here's the best news:

The Best Story Ever is yours

Even if your story has been magnificent up 'til now the best story ever is yet to come.

But… but… but, you say…

My life is in shambles

I've hit rock bottom

I can't make it one more day

To which, I say:

Awesome!

And before you get the chance to ask me if I've lost my mind, I remind you:

The Best Story Ever Starts That Way

Think about it. Don't we cheer for the hero of the best story ever, when all seems lost, when it appears there is no chance and he or she is exhausted, left for dead, and hoping that their next breath would be their last?

It's impossible

I just can't do it

Whether we're turning the page or sitting in a theater on the edge of the seat, we're waiting, anticipating, even praying for the hero of the best story ever… While we can't wait to see

What Happens Next

If you're in the depths of despair, have lost it all and can't imagine having the will to go on, then

Congratulations!

In all the best books, best movies and the greatest stories ever told, if not the opening scene, this moment – the moment that you are experiencing, right now – is the pivotal moment in the best story ever. And YOU are the hero.

This is how to start a story that captivates and mesmerizes all who gain access, whether it's around a campfire, seen on the big screen, on stage, television, read in a printed book or online, your situation is among the best scenes in all great stories.

A few of the best scenes from movies exemplifying this type of pivotal moment that quickly come to mind include **Alien, Amélie, Back to the Future, Die Hard, E.T. The Extraterrestrial, Erin Brockovich, Gladiator, Gravity, Harry Potter, Hunger Games, It's a Wonderful Life, Indiana Jones, Jackie Brown, Kill Bill, Lord of the Rings, Rocky, Star Wars, Still Alice, The Matrix, The Princess Bride, The Terminator**, and I could go on and on... and I think you could think of some, too...

Whether your pivotal moment leads to an instantaneous resolution or opens up an entirely new journey to unfold is yet to be seen but one thing's for certain, something far greater than could ever be imagined in that critical point in time lies just beyond.

When all is lost, you are left for dead face-down on the mat and you can barely hear the referee (who sounds somewhat like the Grim Reaper) begins the long count,

One

When you can't find the will to go on and you think you might just be better off dead…

Two

You try to move your body, but can feel it unresponsive…

Three

You review your decision to bet it all on this match, and where did that get you? Here?

Four

You think of all the promises you made… Now, that all is lost…

Five

Your past flashes in your mind; there have been good times and bad…

Six

It feels like it would be okay to let it go. At least death would be the end of the pain.

Seven

One last look before your unsaid, "goodbye," and you're out for good...

Eight

As you find the strength to open a small slit in your eye, the initial blinding flash of light fades and you see...

Nine

Whatever it is that you see in that moment ushers in hope and determination to go on, as you push yourself up from the mat

This is your defining moment, your Number Nine.

Number 9, number 9, number 9...

The crowd goes wild!

WHAT HAPPENS NEXT?

The best story ever is just beginning...

How you feel about yourself greatly influences what will happen as you get up, and show us what the best part of your story will look like.

The better you feel about yourself, the more you will have and be able to give to a troubled world.

If you are not feeling good about who you are as a person, you are more likely to be tired, depressed, feeling as if you are all alone in this world, anxious or unhappy.

How you feel about the person you see when you look in the mirror affects the entire world that surrounds you; your relationships, your career, satisfaction, and overall quality of life.

Here are a dozen questions to ask that can put you on the path of becoming your highest and best enabling you to have more of yourself to share with a world that needs your positive impact.

1. What does my inner voice say about me?

Sometimes our own inner voice is our worst enemy; old recordings that play on in continuous loops touting self-criticism or unworthiness.

You can interrupt the pattern with a strike-that-reverse-it strategy. There are many methods to approach this kind of negative self-talk but I have found that the most immediate and abrupt interruptions and reversal methods work best.

Snap It Out

For instance, wearing a rubber band on your wrist and snapping it immediately when you sense the negative thought. This creates a stopping point.

Next, you want to say (out-loud, if you can) the opposite, positive reinforcement or reframe of the negative thought three times (this can be silently to yourself if you're in a public environment where this might be inappropriate).

You might also consider a simple tapping exercise that I encourage my clients to use that goes like this:

Tap It Out

Let's say your negative thought was, "I'm stupid." Immediately cock your middle finger with your thumb and flick your ear (just like you might do to your little brother, or maybe you grandmother did that to you to interrupt your pattern of behavior, while remembering that this is not punishment, only a strong signal to stop the thought in its tracks).

You don't have to flick your ear but I do suggest that you flick yourself somewhere around the vicinity of your head because this recognizes and identifies the location where the transgression originated. With a little practice you can develop a flicking method that couldn't even be discerned by the unsuspecting public around you.

Then with the same finger that you flicked yourself with, tap the inside center of the palm of your opposite hand repeatedly. While you tap continuously say the negative thought (out-loud, if you can) three times with as much negative emotion associated with the words that you can muster. While you are doing this, imagine seeing the thought travel from your brain to inside the palm of your hand while you are saying the words. Then close your hand tightly, as if you are gripping the thought so as not to release it.

Next, turn over your clenched fist and tap repeatedly at a rapid pace, just like you did before, only this time repeat the opposite supportive positive phrase (out-loud if you can) that counteracts the negative thought. In this case if might be something, like, "I am getting so much smarter and brilliant every day. I'm a genius!" After the third recitation seal the deal by an affirmative closing statement, like, "I love the new me!"

Then, open your hand and let the negative thought fall down to the ground like a rock. Brush the insides of your hands in a cleansing motion and go on about your day a little better than you were before.

Amazingly, the next time that negative thought interrupts your daily life (if at all), you will find that you have less emotional attachment to it. This is an effective method that breaks the pattern and also removes the psychological pain associated with these negative invasions.

This works for my clients – and it will work for you – if you give it a chance.

Some other questions you might ask could be:

2. How positive is my personal outlook?

We all have heard about how we are supposed to maintain a positive mental attitude ad infinitum. But it can sometimes be a challenge top think positively when you're not feeling so good about yourself or life in general.

It's not enough that we are bombarded by life circumstances that may be less than desirable but we are commonly exposed to negative influences that are quite easily monitored and filtered by simply paying attention and taking action to protect your personal space.

Find ways to focus on the positive. Start looking for the silver lining in everything in your life and avoid or eliminate anything that does not resonate with your happiness.

3. Do I open myself to destructive programming?

The phrase Garbage In Garbage Out (GIGO) originally used amongst computer programmers to refer to erroneous programming code or input producing unrecognizable output. We are not that much different; what we allow as input to our central processing unit (CPU) may produce a perception, belief or feeling based on data that may not be in our best interest.

If you want to take control about how you feel about yourself, it is imperative that you take action to control what information your mind has access to and/or how much attention you will give to certain kinds of data.

I routinely get exposed to data that is extremely interesting to my scientific mind. Then I have to ask myself, "Am I willing to dedicate a great deal of my life's work and energy to this topic?" One must manage economy of time, effort and concentration. Learn how to say, "No," to some projects that would be better served by someone else's expertise. Learning to tune out unnecessary input can help reduce the white noise in your thoughts.

You might consider monitoring, filtering or eliminating other input representing vibrational incongruencies, like media, TV, news, magazines, tabloids, etc... Intentionally seek out more sources of positive input from cognitively selected books, web sites, recordings, videos that are more in line with what you want.

4. What is the quality of my relationships?

You can immediately affect the quality of your self-worth by hanging out with a higher quality of friends and associates. Simply stated, ditch the nay-sayers, nervous perfectionists and compulsive conspiracy theorists and begin to surround yourself with more supportive and positive people.

Some people have a toxic effect on your life. You can tell by the way that you feel after you've spent time with them. Ask yourself, "Do I feel better when I'm around them?" Or do they make you feel drained? If they do not make you feel better, then they are not the kind of people that are in your best interest. If they drain you or are toxic, you need to stop spending time with those people.

Start making more time for the people that make you feel better about yourself. This raises the vibration of your personal power bubble.

5. How much gratitude do I exude?

The more thankful that you are for all the things that bring you joy or that you appreciate in your life also raises your self-esteem. To keep from taking things for granted every day, consider taking a daily 2 Minute Gratitude Break.

It's a good way to take out a couple of minutes to reflect on the day's events and activities. In a seated upright position with your feet flat on the floor, arms relaxed on your legs with hands palm up, take a deep breath in through your nose and let it out through your mouth, repeat as you relax… Concentrate on three things that you are grateful about yourself today (they don't have to be big things).

Consider getting a small notebook to record the three things that you are grateful for each day. Review the list by reading it back to yourself out loud and smile. You may be surprised that as you look for the things that you are thankful for, you will find more good things happening in your life as you look for them. m down, then read them out loud.

6. At what level do I maintain strength and honor?

When you do the right thing, keep your word and stay true to what you believe in, you bolster your self-esteem. This makes you even stronger as you feel better about yourself and more confident about whom you are as a human being.

Mean what you say, say what you mean, let your word be your bond. Make your handshake and the words you express be integrous and trustworthy.

If you are in a leadership or influential position, don't tell others what to do (especially if it sounds like judging others or preaching). Instead lead by example. Let others see your good works and allow them to emulate your performance.

Become predictably dependable, giving others confidence in your ability to do what you say you will do.

7. Am I a perfectionist?

For the perfectionist, you need to lighten up and learn to let go of your rigid perfectionism.

Consider cutting yourself some slack and you'll be surprised at how much more you accomplish in your life which will also make you feel better and better.

It is better to get a thing done, than to do nothing from fear of not being able to complete it perfectly (or procrastination).

Perfectionists have a tendency to lean towards private self-abuse, condemning themselves for falling short (refer back to #1).

Embrace adequacy when doing a project. For instance, if you need to write a report, give yourself a deadline; a date and a time. When the time is up; you're done. Move one and let it go. You could write and re-write for days... Sure, you could re-edit it at another time, but if you do; create a new deadline and stick to it.

I'm not saying to settle for mediocrity or to compromise your integrity, just to cut yourself some slack... for you. You are amazing and you deserve it. And you might be surprised at how much people appreciate your new level of increased performance.

Perfectionists also tend to expect more from their peers, which tends to be a constant cause of frustration. Learn to be more tolerant and let others do the best they can with the tools that they have (not everyone can be as wonderful as you; and that's okay). Learn to let others be.

I know, it seems impossible... but it gets easier.

8. What if I Blow it?

You have to stop the self-deprecation. You are no longer allowed to put yourself down for shortcomings.

From now on, you must learn to forgive yourself and learn to let things go (see #1). Some people ride themselves so hard that they get physically sick.

If you blow it, remember that you are a good person and you're getting better every day.

Then take a look at the facts; what made you do what you did? This is an important step, because we all make mistakes, but if we examine the evidence and identify where we broke weak, we are more likely to prevent stumbling again. (At least in this way, because let's face it, we all misstep sometimes. Nobody's perfect.)

Congratulate yourself for figuring it out and make yourself a promise to look out more for yourself in the future. You have just completed another course in what not to do next time.

Always look for the silver lining, use positive reinforcement, forgive yourself, give yourself a big hug and tell your inner self, "I love you. You are awesome." Because you are.

9. How Do I Treat Others?

Helping others makes you feel better about yourself. Be kind and generous. Commit to random acts of kindness. Volunteer your talent or time to an honorable cause. It feels good to help others who are less fortunate than you.

There's nothing better than The Golden Rule, "Do unto others as you would have them do unto you." No matter what you station in life (even if you feel like you're at the bottom), there's always somebody worse off than you.

I know that I help people every day, and some days... when I feel like I have nothing to give (yes, even I have my down days), but when I force myself to go through the motions on the behalf of someone else; it helps me to resonate with my strength and I get re-charged when my life affects someone else's in a positive manner.

Just a simple compliment can make someone's day, makes you feel better, and others feel better about you, too.

10. When's the last time I tried something new?

Doing something you've never done before (especially something you may have avoided because the thought of it made you uncomfortable) builds self-esteem.

It can be something that you've always wanted to do, or maybe something that may not have even occurred to you.

As you look for opportunities to experience something new, they will appear before you... and engaging in these activities – even it if turns out that you don't like them – gives you self-confidence and assurance in yourself.

It is better to say, "No thanks. I tried it and didn't like it," than to shy away, just because you've never done it before. (Note: this does not apply to illegal activities, which would be contrary to your strength and honor. See #6.)

11. Do I Compare Myself to Others?

Most of the clients I attract are upwardly mobile, focused and committed to high levels of personal excellence and they do tend to struggle with comparing themselves to others. Simply stated, comparing yourself to others drains your personal power.

So what, if someone's better at something than you are? Guess what? You're better at something than someone else. Instead of trying to beat out that person's performance in that area, congratulate them on their strength in that area and move on.

Appreciate others for their unique abilities and you embrace your uniqueness.

Use healthy modeling. When you see in someone else an attribute that you would like to adopt as your own – go ahead – set a goal to attain it for yourself. Try it on; if it doesn't feel comfortable, no problem. You can still have access to that attribute in your life by outsourcing it.

Make a friend or hire a professional that has that attribute as their innate skill.

If you compare yourself to anyone, compare who you are today to whom you were yesterday and continue to grow, measure your growth regularly and applaud your progress.

12. Who could I be?

Whoever you want to be: Be that!

Your path of personal growth is constant and never ending. You are continually growing, changing, reinventing, recreating and expanding into the new, improved you.

As an author, I am discouraged sometimes about the trail of documentation that I leave behind me that is a constant reminder of who I was yesterday. Does that slow me down? No way; onward and upward I go!

Don't get stuck in the past and resist letting it drag you back from whence you came.

Model your mentors and heroes, act as if. I hear you saying, "You mean to fake it?" Yes, fake it 'til you make it. It what everyone learns to do; royalty learns to act like royalty by "acting the part," just like an actor plays a part. As his or her highness is adequately groomed and coached, they appear to be the person they are supposed to be.

When they feel that sense of 100% congruency with whom they are supposed to be; who knows? (Truth be known, they may never feel worthy of the role that they play.)

Dress nicer, groom yourself better and smile. Celebrate the you who is everything that you could be and remember that no matter how far you've come it can be even better.

Invite a glowing self-image by pretending that you have the highest self-esteem ever, and this feeling will find a home to live within you.

Self-esteem is basically how you feel about yourself as a person. It's not so much focused on your competence or abilities as your inner dialogue and feeling about yourself, the things you do and how you do them.

Low Self Esteem

It's not good or bad to have low or high self-esteem, it is what it is and we're all doing the best we can with what we have. Nonetheless, the people I work with find it beneficial to build their self-esteem because it seems to be associated with a certain degree of worthiness.

Good things happen to good people and the better you feel about the good things in your life, the more good things will come to you. Call it what you want, wishful thinking, pop science or new age mumbo jumbo, regardless statistics verify this at a high level of accuracy.

An example might be, let's say you have had the opportunity to apply paint to paper or canvas in such a way as to result in an artistic rendering. You put it up on the wall and say to yourself, "Oh, jeeze, I wish I had better skills then this thing might be worth looking at."

Before you have a chance to take it down, a friend shows up unexpectedly and notices your painting, "Oh, my," he/she says, "I didn't know you painted. That's really nice, you have real talent."

You might reply, "Oh, that? That's nothing. I was just experimenting. Sometimes I wish I could paint, so I dabble, only to discover I can't." While you think to yourself, "Ugh, I suck at this. I don't even know why I did it in the first place."

Your friend assures you that it looks marvelous and that you may have more talent than you give credit to yourself and departs. You take down the painting and berate yourself, while thinking that your friend was only saying those things in an effort to be nice.

If you have low self-esteem you're likely to be your own worst critic, with a self-loathing voice often disrespecting you, your value and any good you could possibly bring to the world. Even if you've accomplished a good thing, there is little sense of accomplishment (as if you'd barely gotten through it at all) and certainly no celebration or sense of pride in a job well done. And if someone attempts to validate your efforts by paying a compliment, you're likely to discard it.

Somewhere at the root of lack of self-esteem, is feeling that you're not good enough.

Yet, there is an innate part of us that aspires to feel good, so we try to feel the void of not feeling good with other things that will make us feel better or distract us from our own self-deprecation.

People with low self-esteem attempt to fill the void with accomplishments, social status, fancy things, degrees, wealth, surrounding one's self with influential people, thrill-seeking, extra-marital affairs, feeding addictions such as alcohol, drugs and/or food, etc. only to find the underlying feeling of unworthiness remains.

Comparison

Often how we feel about ourselves is based upon our inner system of weights and balances used when comparing ourselves to other people.

When you look at someone else, do you believe that you are as attractive, intelligent, successful, deserving of love and happiness as anyone else?

If your tendency is to feel as though you are less of a person than someone else, then you will be prone to deliberate compromises that are not in your best interests, such as being a people pleaser, submissive, a perfectionist, suffer from mood imbalances, depression, even more unworthiness or a compulsion to prove that we are somehow better than someone else or they are undeserving.

High Self Esteem

If you are blessed to have high self-esteem, it was likely the result of your familial or social upbringing that influenced your sense of not only being good enough, but deserving of all the best things this life has to offer. For the most part, this is the story of your life. You are one of the good people that good things keep happening to.

You might have been raised in an environment that supported a high perceived value of self in respect to family, love, religion, friendships, team sports or other relationships. When surrounded by your circle of influence you are ecstatically empowered; this sense of worthiness and power is ingrained enough to carry you through most anything.

Then there are those who have achieved high self-esteem based on performance or competency. These are those who invest their efforts to support their family, their professions or the community at large and feel a strong sense of worthiness based on the kind of person they are and the things they do.

The downside to high self-esteem, is running the risk of being viewed by others as selfish, conceited, arrogant, or narcissistic; so tempering high self-esteem with humility produces a healthier balance overall.

Building Self Esteem

The first place to start is to recognize your inner voice eschewing any sense of worthiness you might have. Listen for your self-talk and stop it. In the style of the late, Gene Wilder in Willy Wonka and the Chocolate Factory, "Strike that. Reverse it." Then repeat to yourself just the opposite.

Think about it this way; I think we all can agree within us resides a small-child version of ourselves. If we could imagine inviting that little person out to stand in front of us and say to that child the negative things we say to ourselves, it would likely drive that little person to tears. We would never say those kinds of things to a child. What would we do instead? We would offer words of encouragement, edifying and uplifting the child for doing the best he/she could and you affirm the results were magnificent based on their level of performance and even alludes to possible greatness. Right?

It doesn't matter what other people say. What matters is what you say to you. When you feel negative thoughts this is your cue to give yourself some loving support. Stop berating yourself.

The next thing to do is to start acting as if you have high self-esteem.

If you have high self-esteem:

- You know you are worthy of all the best things this life has to offer
- You take good care of yourself
- You help others, but only after tending to your own needs first
- You take care of your body, eat well, exercise and have good sleep habits
- You manage your time well
- You set boundaries in respect to yourself
- You find excuses to celebrate and have fun
- You are financially responsible. You spend less than you earn, save and invest
- You are confident in your skills and abilities
- If you fall short, you do not beat yourself up over it
- You take personal responsibility for everything in your life
- You are the manager of your emotional state
- You readjust and reaffirm the best things in life the best you can considering the current circumstances (which could be dire)
- You do not allow your appearance, circumstances, status, social interactions, wealth or relationships to dictate your emotional state
- Nor do you rely on addictive behaviors to affect your state of being

These are the goals to set and achieve as you build self-esteem, and as you practice these attributes they will become more and more a part of who you are. You will fall in love with the magnificent person you are – and always have been – and enjoy the presence of the person reflected in your mirror.

Celebrate!

Every now and then good stuff happens… and it's easier to document now, more than ever. Most everyone has a cellphone with a camera built in. I'm still getting adjusted to all this communication technology, where we're all more connected digitally, thanks to the high-tech gadgets and apps that keep coming out regularly.

Even though my kids live out-of-town, we can keep in contact in real-time and I absolutely love sharing in all the little celebrations, no matter what they are or where they are.

I share in their wins, celebrating with them, and share the celebrations with my friends, like, "there's a party going on right here…"

It is so important to celebrate all the things that happen in your life – even if they are small wins – you should celebrate them in a big way.

Why?

Because celebrating your wins enthusiastically acts like a happiness magnet. The more you celebrate the good stuff, the more good stuff comes to you.

Celebration Hack

Here's a hot tip to supercharge your happiness, goodness and life moments worth celebrating:

Celebrate Enormously

If your celebration attracts more celebratory events, it stands to reason (and it's true) the more enthusiastically you celebrate, the better the events to celebrate that are attracted for you to celebrate.

The benefits of exaggerated celebrating include the increased biochemical release of hormones like Dopamine, Serotonin, Oxytocin and Endorphins. It's the perfect cocktail for a natural high, with the added benefit of attracting even more of the same. Based on your enthusiasm, you can expect even more in both frequency and volume.

I Don't Feel Like Celebrating

It's understandable that when you're feeling blue or under the weather, you may not feel like celebrating much. This is when it's most important to muster up as much celebratory ambition as possible, because of the whole attraction-thing.

When something good happens worth celebrating, even if it's not about you (it might be something good that's happened to someone else, like your friend, child, grandchild, relative or even a celebrity) just the act of sharing someone else's good fortune helps to release the celebration hormone cocktail. So, brace yourself…

We're gonna have a good time tonight

Let's celebrate, it's all right

Even if you cannot manage to be feeling very happy at the outset, sharing it with someone who has more capacity to embrace someone else's celebration, helps release more celebration hormones within you, like a happiness virus, it doesn't take long and you're feeling much better.

Want even more?

No problem, find someone else to share the same information with, next thing you know you're a full-on celebration machine!

And as you ramp up all that celebratory enthusiasm, you know what happens next:

Ya-hoo!

Here comes even more stuff to celebrate

Comin' down the pike

Say, "Goodbye," to your funk and, "Hello," to your new life of enthusiastic celebration.

So bring your good times and your laughter too

We gonna celebrate and party with you

(Thanks to Kool and the Gang for the celebration soundtrack.)

7

EMBRACE JOY AND HAPPINESS

Enjoy feeling good about living a better life by being one of the good people

Five easy steps leading to you're enjoying the best this life has to offer, sharing your goodness with others as we all do a little something-something to make the world a better place.

Be Good

Smile. Treat others with kindness, respect and tolerance. A little tolerance goes a long way. Do not judge other people, their actions. If you feel the inclination to look down at someone, make fun of them or feel anger or resentment welling up inside you, try to put yourself in the other person's shoes and imagine what it must be like to be living their life. Realize that they, just like you, are doing the best they can with what they have. Empathize and send them love instead.

Focus on Good Things

Look for and see the good in all things. Even in the worst of times, be looking for the beauty, the love, the positivity that abounds in all situations, even when it's difficult to imagine anything good at the time. Do not research, look at, read, listen to or engage in conversation about injustice, tragedy, natural disaster or any other opportunities to be caught up in a whirlpool of negativity. Listen to music that makes you happy (not sad songs), read Chicken Soup for the (fill in the blank) Soul books or any other book that is implicitly positive. Look at images that fill your heart with joy, post them around your house, on Facebook (don't share anything negative) and at work.

Be Around Good People

The people you surround yourself with carry and maintain a particular vibration. If they have a negative vibration, it is difficult – if not impossible – for them to see the good in any situation. This negative vibration permeates the space around these individuals and is infectious to others. Being around people who talk about or focus on negativity or things that are wrong or bad in the world, lower your vibration. Enough exposure will drag your vibration down to match theirs.

Likewise, spending more time around more positive people who maintain higher, more optimistic vibrations will elevate your vibration to match theirs, as you are in their presence more often. Find new friends who have higher vibrations. Being around good people, who are optimistic, use good words and do good things makes positivity easier.

Do Good Things

Start finding ways to do things that are good. Unsolicited acts of kindness, even if very small, help to make the world a better place. Be polite and courteous. Smile and compliment the cashier, let someone who looks like they're in a hurry merge in traffic, let someone go before you in the checkout line, tip the waitress, hold the door for someone with their hands full. Look for opportunities to assist others who might need a helping hand, or just a word of encouragement. Make a donation to a worthy cause, help promote a worthy cause or start a worthy cause of your own (only make sure that it, like you, focuses on something good, not bad).

Feel Good Activities

The more you engage in activities that make you feel good, the better you feel. The better you feel, the easier it is to pass your goodness to others. Doing things that make you feel good raises you vibration and affects the vibration(s) of those around you.

As you feel increasingly better because you're being in the places and participating more in activities that make you feel good, this "good feeling" attracts more good opportunities and circumstances in your life.

21 Day Good Life Challenge

Don't believe me? I dare you to take the 21 Day Good Life Challenge. Take a 21-day negativity hiatus. Determine to be good for three weeks, starting today. Start each day by looking in the mirror and saying, "I love my life!" *(TM Adam Markel)*. Cut out images that make you feel good and stick them around on your mirror. Tolerate more, focus on good things, spend more time around good people, find opportunities to do good things, and make more time to do the things that bring you joy.

Three weeks of living the good life will raise your vibration enough, you will never want to sink back to where you were before as you being to live the life you always wanted to live and enjoy it more fully every day.

The most important component for enjoying a fun-filled life full of happiness and joy is just like magic or anything else: It's easy once you know the secret of the happiness hormone. Once you have this knowledge, the question is

What will you do about it?

Hidden within our molecular structure is a hormone that when released into our bloodstream allows us to experience happiness and joy. The hormone has been identified and named, "oxytocin." There is no pill or supplement that you can take to replace the hormone or trigger its production.

Oxytocin is created naturally during moments of great feelings of love, falling in love and loving orgasm. We experience the greatest happiness when oxytocin levels are at their highest levels. This is why oxytocin is referred to as, "the love hormone."

The higher your level of oxytocin, the happier you are; you feel better, experience less cardiovascular stress, enjoy increased immune system and a longer lifespan with a higher quality of life.

How to Be Happy

Fortunately, there are things that you can do to ramp up your oxytocin levels to increase happiness and joy (besides the obvious: falling in love, engaging in love-filled sex or having a newborn baby).

Only you have the ability to pull the trigger, releasing the happiness hormone, but you must take action to do so.

Here are some things you can do to increase your oxytocin levels post haste:

WATCH A MOVIE

There are two types of films you could watch that will trigger the release of oxytocin. They are movies that make you laugh out loud, or cry tears of joy or sadness.

SOCIAL MEDIA

Yes, engaging and interacting with other people in a positive manner (haters are excluded because "haters gonna hate" indicates increased testosterone – not oxytocin) via social media, like facebook, Twitter, etc... increases the happiness hormone.

DONATE

Making a contribution or donation, expecting nothing in return, is an excellent way to release the happiness hormone.

PRAY

If you're open to prayer/meditation, the idea of interacting with your higher source or self (feel free to call it whatever you want. I am quite comfortable with the idea of praying to God, but to each their own…) this will release oxytocin.

PET AN ANIMAL

If you're so inclined, petting a cute, adorable animal (who is amiable to the idea and not a ferocious man-eating critter) will get those happiness juices flowing.

NATURE WALK

Taking a stroll through natural surroundings, especially on a sunny day, when you can appreciate trees, grass, flowers or a natural body of water or shoreline will do the trick.

GET A MASSAGE

A little trip to the massage therapist for your choice of either a sports or relaxation massage (or a spa day) will do the trick.

Increase Happiness Hormone X2

You can achieve twice the amount of oxytocin release by engaging in activities with another person (also, in most cases, the other person gets similar benefits). Consider:

FULL-ON LISTENING

Talk to someone – or more importantly invite them to talk and share – focusing totally on the speaker and their delivery. Look into their eyes, watch their mouth, note their voice inflection, posture and be aware of their body language. (And for god's sake, turn your cell phone off.)

DO A MEAL

Either take someone out to share a meal – your treat – or make someone a special dinner to share with him or her.

DANCE

Getting out on the dance floor with someone to bust a move is a great way to increase your happiness levels. (And don't worry; it's more about the wiggling to the music than it is your proficiency at dancing. No judges here.)

HAVE A THRILL

Do something that you've never done before – especially if it has a little danger thrown in for flavor – like a roller coaster ride or skydiving.

BE TRUSTED

The feeling that comes with being trusted by another person (not trusting someone else) releases the happiness hormone. Being trustworthy, helps stack the deck in your favor.

SAY, "I LOVE YOU."

Every time you communicate your admiration for another person, using the words, "I love you," works just like an injection of oxytocin.

HUGGING

Doctor's orders a daily prescription of 8 hugs per day to keep your hug quotient at its optimal levels.

Happy Happiness

Enjoy these little activities that can give you a happy life.

May each day be your happiest day ever.

Keep in mind, you can find things to do to increase your happiness quotient without having to spend a lot of money.

When someone has let their finances get out of control and is trying to get a handle on their cash flow one of the first concerns is reductions in quality of life. The novice budgeter is likely to assume that maintaining a strict budget will mean having no fun.

While your new budget may only have a minimal amount set aside for entertainment, it only means that your former more expensive entertainment will be curtailed. You can have so much fun without having to spend too much, and you might be surprised to discover hours of enjoyment from activities that are even free.

While this list is far from complete, it is only offered as an idea springboard to get you thinking about entertainment in different ways, realizing that just because you're on a budget doesn't mean you can't have fun. As a matter of fact, it is important to have as much cheap or free fun as possible while you're reeling-in your expenditures.

Free things to do

Free Community Events

Check the local newspaper or online magazine for free events happening in your local area. Local organizations often sponsor free activities for residents. Find out what's happening near you.

Visit the Library

Remember libraries? Though they are fading away, they are still around. You can easily spend hours perusing the treasures at your local library. Plus, this is an excellent free location to meet others at as an alternative to a restaurant and they may have a separate meeting area for you to use… for free.

Explore Your Local Outback

Find natural areas to explore not far from where you live. Take a hike, go geocaching, walk around the lake, frolic at the park, feed the birds, party at the beach or have a picnic.

Party at Home

You can start your own at-home event, invite friends and host a murder mystery game, karaoke night, poker night, open mic night (sing, play an instrument, read poetry, standup comedy, etc.). Make it a potluck and an evening of it.

Create a Book with Friends

Join with friends to create a recipe book, or collection of stories, Chicken Soup for the Soul-style, or otherwise. Publish it in Amazon's Kindle format and donate the proceeds to a good cause.

Book Club

Get a group of folks together who agree to read a particular book in tandem, one chapter per week. Meet somewhere in person, virtually, online or via a free conference call to discuss insights from the chapter.

Book Exchange

Host a book exchange, where you and avid book readers each bring a box of books and an hors d'oeuvre appetizer to exchange with other readers. Exchange meeting could be held at home or an off-site location.

Host a White Elephant Exchange

Everyone gift wraps and brings an unwanted gift they have received from someone else (within a specified price-range) at some point in time and exchange them (in a variety of ways). It's fun and everyone leaves with something.

Get Dirty

If you have access to some dirt at home or nearby, cultivate a garden or weed community landscapes. Many people enjoy the feel of the earth in their hands while nurturing the planet.

Go Dumpster Diving

If you're like me, this will probably never be on your radar, but I have come across so many people who absolutely love dumpster diving (don't worry, I won't mention your names) and you'd be surprised to hear some of the treasures they've uncovered doing so.

Start a Collection

Start a collection of something without cost, like drink coasters, rocks, shells, glass, feathers, bugs, themed photo collections, etc...

Barter for Entertainment

If you have a particular skill set (which we all do) you may offer to trade your services with any purveyor of recreational activity you like, in exchange for partaking in their offering. Good for anything from fancy restaurants and concert tickets to high end lodging and cruises.

Walk the Dog

Obvious for someone who has a dog, but if you don't have a dog, you could sign up via the SPCA to walk someone else's dog.

Start a Blog

Have a passion or opinion that you would like to share with the community at large. Start a blog. It's free. You can post as often as you like and get the word out about what's important to you.

Learn Something New

You can teach yourself just about anything these days, just by pouring over data from Google searches or viewing hours upon hours of free how-to videos on YouTube.

Volunteer

Give some of your time or talent to bless others via your local community organizations, or offer to mow the lawn for a neighborhood widow, you get out, plus you're helping to make the world a better place.

Express Gratitude

Make a list of all the people who have been a blessing to you at some point in their life, and send them a note, email, private message thanking them for inspiring you. Include anyone from grade school teachers and friends to celebrities and family members. (Maybe write a memoir delineating their positive influence.)

8

TOLERANCE AND SABBATICALS

Tolerate Much?

When you see someone going through a difficult situation, or having trouble navigating their life path or suffering an enormous misfortune, as though they were thrashing through the brush with a machete the whole way, what are your thoughts?

Do you think,

A – What a freak (or alternatively),

> **They should get a life**, or
> **If they'd been through what I've been through…**

B – I wonder what it's like to be in that person's shoes?

Immediately, you get the idea that I've set you up, to give you a choice of selecting either disrespect or empathy. Honestly, though, what is your knee-jerk reaction? I hear a lot of people being disrespectful.

You might be surprised, if I were to ask those same people if faced with a similar situation *(just the same, only different)* their reply would be to unequivocally stand on the idea that their first response would be one of empathy.

An interesting observation, don't you think?

It's no wonder it's so difficult for people to get along with each other these days.

Tolerance is the ability, skill or innate psychological behavior of allowing others to be the way they are, regardless of whether it is in contrast with you. And the best type of tolerance is celebrating that people are the way they are, and that's okay.

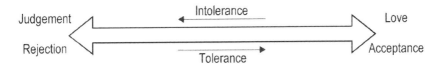

If tolerance is considered to be a spectrum, on the left-hand side of the spectrum there would be judging and rejection, on the other end would be love and acceptance. Certainly there are a myriad of tolerant or intolerant behaviors and attitudes in between those two extremes.

Why are we likely to be intolerant?

Because we've been programmed that way since birth; our parents, their parents, public schools, our peers, the media, and now with social media and immediate access to information via the World Wide Web, our first reaction is to reject and alienate others.

To laugh at their misfortune, make fun of their condition, call them ugly, fat, disgusting, ignorant or stupid.

Oh, it's hilarious (you might think) but what's really going on in that viral video clip?

You don't know... or is it that you don't care?

This leads me to believe that there exists a conspiracy promoted by the powers that be to keep us divided, to intentionally pit us one against the other, in an effort to keep us weak and dependent on the government for assistance. And they're fueling the fire of polarization, like no one's business.

Don't believe me?

If you're on Facebook, take a look at your feed. See any dissention there? What videos are popular on YouTube? Anyone watch the nightly news lately?

Then there's You and Me

Maybe we're the only ones, the two of us; together we could agree to be more tolerant, to try to understand others as we would like to be understood and accepted for all our talents and inadequacies on our good days and bad days.

After all, aren't we all just doing the best we can with what we have?

The next step in human evolution is tolerance. ***Tolerance = Love***[n]

Intolerance is illogical

To be intolerant, doesn't even make good sense.

It's as if, when engaged in the activity of judging or ridiculing someone else, the person who is doing it can't even see the hypocrisy in their doing so... How do we find congruency at all in this degree of superiority and isolation?

Even now, as you read these words, there are some who are locked, loaded and ready to attack me, twist my words and suggest that I am promoting some kind of crazy campaign. This is not addressed to them.

This is addressed to you: That **one other person**, who along with me is making a commitment to be more tolerant... because to you and me, it makes more sense to treat others as we would like to be treated.

Are you with me?

Take a Sabbatical

Sometimes in life amidst the pursuit of success and happiness it is prudent, if not necessary to take a break from the constant grind of your daily routine and completely unplug from your profession for a period of time to re-center, evaluate, reposition yourself and consider charting an entirely new course for your life's journey.

This process takes more than the traditional week or two of vacation and can take months or years. Corporations are seeing the value of this increasing employee or partner value over time and may offer official sabbaticals (extended separation or leave with, or without, pay while not losing their job as they take this important personal time to focus on themselves free from professional constraints).

In some cases, if taking an authorized sabbatical is not an option, one may have to resign completely and walk away.

If you have been stuck in a particular career path for many years, you may need more time to effectively separate, discover and reconnect with your true self. In many cases our sense of self erodes or dissolves away in service to others, especially over long periods of time. Everyone is different, some may require months off to conduct their rediscovery, for others, it could take years.

Being restrained in an intense, high-pressure profession is manageable but over time the stress and strain can understandably take a toll on even the most top performance professional, leading some on a crash course to burnout, or worse, even to suicidal thoughts and tendencies. How much better would it be to take a break (sabbatical) with the likelihood of returning to your profession re-exhilarated and ready to conquer the world?

The better you prepare for your break, the less concerned you will be about the day-to-day responsibilities (part of the purpose of the break). Have some money set aside in savings. Investigate health care or insurance options, maintenance of retirement accounts and other accounts while you remain unplugged.

I had a client who lacking any preparation (but felt it was imperative to take immediate action) quit his job without notice, moved to a small coastal community, lived in a trailer and washed dishes at a restaurant to finance his break. He says it not only saved his life, but empowered him to discover new meaning and purpose in his life. (You might be surprised if you knew who was working in the kitchen at the restaurant you frequent.)

Now, he is back on the top of his game, more successful and better than ever following his three-year severance. I know many people who have self-financed their sabbatical via Internet Marketing, where all they needed was an Internet-capable device and an Internet connection... and they never went back to traditional work environment.

Even so, you might consider better preparation for your sabbatical, including plans to return in some fashion, shape or form. It's best not to burn any bridges upon your departure from service.

What you do during this extended time off is totally up to you. What is important self-focused, self-indulgent, self-sacrificing or inner exploration of self is totally individualized for each person. Do not fashion your break after anyone else's, nor compare your break to anyone else's. Even though you may use someone else's break for inspiration and may even begin modeling after someone's sabbatical that went before, let your journey unfold and change direction to better suit your own inner work, personal needs and desires.

Take this time to rediscover who you are, your inner being… Connect, or reconnect, with your life's purpose, your individual mission and message to bring to the world. Find your authentic voice from within and celebrate by singing your song.

Focus on your individualized healing, incorporating rest and relaxation. Engage in activities that thrill you, bring a sense of joy to your soul or give you a strong sense of purpose or meaning. Take this precious time to accomplish some of the items you might love to scratch off of your bucket list.

This is your time to be or do anything you want. Consider travelling to a new location, engaging in a new field of study or trying out new hobbies. Experiment with new recreational activities and technologies, whatever piques your interest, try it; see if you like it.

Expect to emerge like the Phoenix from the ashes. The new you will be more able to achieve more, be more and offer more to the local community and the world at large than ever before.

9

WHAT'S LOVE GOT TO DO WITH IT?

In my opinion the sad truth of the deterioration of romantic love in our society is tragic.

Just as everything in the mainstream is moving toward making everything disposable diapers, water bottles, razors, pens, tissues, plates, shower curtains and home furnishings, likewise people and romantic relationships are also becoming more and more disposable.

I have witnessed this transition take place. I've seen the budding marriages forged in the fifties, fall victim to the wild abandon of the sixties. Then, in the seventies, the legal system welcomed no fault divorces ushering in the disposable marriage that has led to where we are today, bruised, broken and unable to find any love inside.

I never asked the question, "What is love?" because as far back as I can remember, I had a keen inner sense or knowing what love meant to me, and even though I could have followed my peers in the sexual revolution, I maintained my composure and waited for "the one" I would marry following high school.

Innately, I always had an integrous approach to not only keep my word, but especially to do so if I made a vow of commitment in front of family and friends as witnesses. I pledged my love and commitment to not only a woman, but a family and the community. To me, this was heavy business, as love is a terrible thing to waste.

My deep respect for integrous love is one of the many things contributing to my personal freakiness. I don't mind admitting it, and I proudly let my freak flag fly. I'd much rather make my own way, forge my own trail, research and discover new ideas, enjoy fulfillment, happiness and a quality of life that eludes the masses.

When I began my journey in the God business, I focused on love and relationships (no surprise, as this was my passion, even wrote a book about it) only to find the people who were attracted to counsel with me were not as interested in healing their relationship. Instead of asking, "How can we make our relationship better?" they were asking, "How do you know when your marriage is over?"

If you are in a potentially amazing romantic relationship, yet constantly on guard, continually looking for signs your marriage is over, chances are you will find what you are looking for. In fact, we know this to be true; you do find what you are looking for (and you always find it in the last place you look).

When someone comes in for relationship counsel asking, "Is my marriage over?" why we don't just affirm, "Yes, you've already aligned yourself with the idea that love doesn't exist, therefore it does not, and your marriage is over." Cut your losses now, seek an attorney, get everything you can and be done with it as quickly and inexpensively as possible.

One of the main reasons I shifted my focus from relationships, was because my relationship ministry appeared to be more like torture. If someone is looking for an escape route, planning when to leave a marriage is appropriate. If he or she is thinking about how to end a marriage, then the best intentions of any counselor, therapist, coach or cleric has very little to work with. The best you can hope for is to delay the inevitable which usually leads to more damage, hurt feelings and increased legal battles. Where's the love in that?

The only people who make out on that deal are the relationship counselors, divorce lawyers and the domestic division of our legal system that supports the whole relationship debacle. (Don't get me started on the decline of that system…)

I knowingly share the realization of the truth of what is, and I say, "I still believe in true love." I believe that true love is making its way back to us. I'm not saying that it's not (note to editors: the double-negative was intentional) going to be a difficult journey, especially when I look around and survey all the broken people with little capacity for love at all within them (more about that, later…).

Our lack of respect for integrous love has left an indelible mark on our hearts, if it hasn't stomped out any hope of romantic love for good, but there is a growing compulsion that is beginning to emerge as people realize that all this independence is not what it's cracked up to be.

True love does exist, there is love waiting for you that is difficult for you to imagine in this moment, and you don't have to worry about how to find true love, because it will find you. This life, in its highest form is all about love, and you will never be happier and fulfilled as when you change your perspective and begin to peer through the eyes of love.

Think about opening your heart to love… Not just romantic love (that may be too much to ask, from where you are at the moment), but dare to begin to look at anything, beginning with the smallest of things, then progress to other situations and circumstances, with love in your heart.

You will be surprised at how you attract even more love, the more your love light shines from within. It's a process you can love…

Love is a vibration that when activated acts like a magnet to attract good things to you. Most of us can only maintain the love vibration for short periods of time, due to the interruptions and distractions altering our vibration to lower levels.

Love and Above

The longer you can maintain the Love vibration opportunities will abound for increasing your vibrational state even higher. Higher states of vibration include Joy, Peace and Enlightenment.

Striving to maintain the love vibration will attract more love to you like a magnet. You will have more opportunities to love and bless others with your high love frequency. Plus, as a love magnet, you will have the benefit of being closer to even higher frequencies putting joy, peace and enlightenment more readily within reach.

If you imagined your vibration as a spectrum on a number line from 1 to 1,000, Love would populate the center point with a value of 500, to the right would be Joy, Peace and Enlightenment, to the left in descending order would be Logic, Forgiveness, Optimism, Trust, Courage, Pride, Anger, Want, Fear, Grief, Hopelessness, Guilt and Misery.

| 20 | 30 | 50 | 75 | 100 | 125 | 150 | 175 | 200 | 250 | 310 | 350 | 400 | 500 | 540 | 600 | 700+ |

Misery – Guilt – Hopelessness – Grief – Fear – Want – Anger – Pride – Courage – Trust – Optimism – Forgiveness – Understanding – Love – Joy – Peace – Enlightenment

The spectrum of emotional vibrations on this chart includes the following emotional markers for vibrational states from low level vibration to higher levels of vibratory states:

Misery – Guilt – Hopelessness – Grief – Fear – Want – Anger – Pride – Courage – Trust – Optimism – Forgiveness – Logic – Love – Joy – Peace – Enlightenment

Each vibratory state will have a tendency to move to a neighboring state, either higher or lower, creating a standard range. The interruption or distraction disrupting your current state could either plummet or ramp up your vibrational state instantly, depending on the situation, circumstance and/or your emotional response to the disruption.

Most of us, when learning about the death of a loved one would instantly sink to the depths of low-level vibrations, while winning the lottery would rapidly send us higher up the vibrational chart.

Each of us maintains a standard range of emotional vibration, though this range may change periodically throughout your life, depending on the stage of your life in time and space and your relationship with the world.

The prudent life traveler on his/her journey seeks to manage his or her vibratory emotional state, with the intent on raising their standard range of vibration up the chart. My standard range varies between 200 and 500, but

I am working on living a better life with a tighter range of 400 to 600 or more. It is a process and just like any other skill in this life, learning to manage one's emotional state and vibration can be learned, though it is highly individual. So, what works for one traveler may not work the same way for someone else on a different journey.

Whether there exists a worldwide conspiracy to cause regular disruptions to your vibrational state is debatable. The fact remains for those who are focussing on raising their vibration, it appears as though any number of circumstances or influences can break a higher vibration, this could include interaction with other people or exposure to negative media reports among an endless supply of negativity surrounding the general populous.

10

TELL YOUR STORY
WRITE YOUR BOOK

Rarely does a day go by that someone doesn't ask me about writing their book. There is no doubt – *and I firmly believe* – that every person whose heart yet beats has a book inside them dying to get out. The key is allowing the book to be born before you die.

I'm not just randomly saying you need to get your book out before you die because it sounds like a catchy phrase. I'm saying that because I am holding in my hands – *right now* – the unpublished manuscript from a client and friend who has passed away and it disturbs me greatly.

One's life is comprised of not just a single story, but many stories potentially beneficial to the community at large… or at the very least, preserving your thoughts in your voice, in effect leaving something meaningful behind. And for god's sake, don't wait until it's too late.

People approach me because part of what I do is to help people tell their stories, transitioning to published author. As the author of the out-of-print book, *7-day Author: You Can Write and Publish Your Book in 7 Days*, somehow people still get their hands on the book and contact me. *7 Day Author* is no longer relevant due to huge changes in book publishing since the book was released. I still assist clients and friends in telling their stories, writing their books and publishing them within a week, although it is done entirely differently now.

Why don't I revise the book? The fact is, the industry changes rapidly (as many do) and to commit to a book that may lose relevance or go out of print when the shift happens is no longer a compelling motivation for me. So, now I focus on writing books that are more evergreen, having a longer shelf-life and relevancy.

Story of My Life

Back to your story, the story of your life, stories or life's lessons yearning to be told. When is now a good time to take action?

You never know what life will bring. Every day I thank God for another chance to continue living this life, doing my part –in some (even small) way – to help make the world a better place and to fulfill my life's purpose of helping others achieve their highest and best.

Hopefully, as you read these words, you are also listening to that voice within beseeching you to, *"Please write our story."* The only difference between authors and those who are not authors is that the authors took the action(s) necessary to write and publish their words.

Yes, I do help people write their books for a fee, but it is not my intent to sell you anything, as there are many ways to write and publish your book at little or no cost to you. It's not about me, it's about you; your story that must be told. It's up to you to take the action...

Start writing. Use pen or pencil and paper, type on a typewriter, use a computer or your cell phone. You could even get a digital (or tape) recorder and simply speak your words and either transcribe them yourself, have someone else do it or use your computer as a transcription device using something, like Dragon Speak. However you do it, do something... every day. You will be surprised how a few hundred words a day will accrue into what could become your book, which may include an important message that needs to be told. In fact, it may be *the reason* you have lived the life that you have lived.

How to Write a Book

The "how" in how to write a book is of less concern to you in this moment than the actual writing of your book. The most important first step requires taking the daily action of recording your thoughts. This is more important than not doing it.

I believe every person has many books within themselves, hidden away. There is no reason for you to not share your life and stories with the world. I help people write books about all kinds of things, but writing a book about your life is often the launching point exercise to begin your writing career. In most cases, once you see the basic story of your life in print, all the stories begin to bubble up within your soul begging to be released in your next book.

When I work with someone on their book about their life, we usually (depending on the client's availability, participation and schedule) get this written and published within one week. Just by modeling what I do with my clients, you can do the same thing and follow along with my process.

Now, you, too, will know

How to Write a Book about Your Life

THE PROCESS

Don't Have a Process.

I have learned over time, that being organized (or too organized) can deal the death-blow to writing the story of your life.

All I do is to get you, the burgeoning author, on the phone and talk to you at length about your life. The entire interview is recorded. No pattern, no process, just rambling on in free-flowing style, recording everything.

It's no different than talking to a friend about your life.

Step #1: Tell the Stories about Your Life

Simply talk it out and record it on any voice recording device you have... No notes, no agenda, just ramble on. If something is out of order, no worries, just keep recording and mention, "Oh, yeah, I forgot that before we went to Disneyland, we stopped by this restaurant to eat and we all left without paying for our food. Not that we did it on purpose, we were just so exciting about going to Disneyland that nobody thought about it. The only time I ever did a 'dine and dash,' though unintentionally." Just keep going.

Step #2: Transcribe Your Stories

Next you've got to get your spoken word into an electronic text format. There are many methods for transcribing voice recordings to text, use any one you want. It is likely there is a transcriptionist you can hire locally, or you can find these services easily online.

Step #3: Sort Your Stories

With all your stories separated into individual pieces, now you can go about putting them in the proper sequence.

Formulating your ideas into chapters and having a beginning, a middle and an end may be something you can handle, though it is always good to enlist the aid of someone to assist in the formatting, proofreading and editing, if that is possible. If not, don't let it stop you. Speaking of stopping:

DON'T LET ANYTHING STOP YOU

Don't second-guess yourself, do not allow self-doubt to creep up, don't let any sense of unworthiness threaten your progress. You don't need to be famous, have a fancy degree or even adequate writing skills to tell your story. You only need to tell it and let nothing stand between you and the publishing of your book.

Step #4: I Almost Forgot

This can go on forever, so forget endless editing. Step four is for light editing just to fill in any of the missing pieces that might seem apparent to the reader.

Commit to getting this project completed. You can always go back and change it later, if you have to... Or (better yet) come out with a Volume 2, because more often than not, there is much more about your life to be told, which will continue to occur to you along the way. Record it for the next one.

Step #5: Create Your Manuscript

Create a single electronic document, with title page, etc... There are free templates that can be downloaded online for you to use, though they are not expressly necessary, as the most progressive publishers of the day, like Amazon, have made it very easy for you to get this done, as they do much of the heavy lifting.

Step #6: Publish Your Book

Now, thanks to Amazon, publishing the book about your life is easy, making the story of your life instantly available to anyone in the world (with access to Amazon, or any major bookseller). Simply create an account and upload your manuscript to Amazon's instant printed book division at www.createspace.com.

It is quicker and easier to publish your book today – *now* – more than ever. Once you have your manuscript you can publish it freely in both eBook (Kindle) format and physical printed books (the kind you can hold in your hands and sit on your bookshelf) on demand via Amazon.

Don't worry about cover art for your book unless you have already had someone create individual art for your book cover because Create Space provides many templates for you to choose from and you can easily upload and have placed into the existing template a cover photo and/or author's photo.

Step #7: Celebrate Your Book!

Be the first person to order your book. Once your package arrives: *Celebrate!*

You are now a published author... and if you're anything like those who also done the same thing... Now, you're just getting started.

NO EXCUSES

There is no reason you cannot get this done. Dear God, please don't let your opportunity to tell your story – in your words – lapse.

We and the world are waiting...

Even now, we are listening for your voice, desiring to read your words...

SHARE YOUR BOOK

If you have taken the action to get your message out and write your book, please let me know, so that I can share it with others who can be encouraged by your decisiveness in taking the action to see your thoughts documented and come to life.

ABOUT THE AUTHOR

David M. Masters is an author, speaker, coach, consultant and trainer who's mission in life is to help others achieve their highest and best.

His personal journey has led him throughout a wide spectrum of professions, while maintaining his mission with tenacity and love.

Masters often corrects those who refer to him as a motivational speaker with the distinction, "I am not a motivational speaker but I do attract and work with a more motivated audience."

His is enjoying the lives of his magical children, all who are manifesting incredible lives and making the world a better place.

He currently resides in the Pacific Northwest and can be found frolicking with his grandchildren in his spare time.

For more information, see: www.davidmmasters.com

Note: This book includes an excerpt from Success Attributes © 2008 David M Masters

Made in the USA
San Bernardino, CA
27 September 2016